CREATED FOR MORE

DESTINY IMAGE BOOKS BY PAUL E. TSIKA

Created for More: Discovering God's Transforming Grace

What You Seed Is What You Get: Seeding Your Way to Success

Dream Doer: Dream Building Secrets from the Life of Noah

The Overcomer's Edge: Strategies for Victorious Living in 13 Key Areas of Life

The Language of Leadership: It's More Than Just Talk (audiobook)

Growing in Grace: Daily Devotions for Hungry Hearts (audiobook) with Billie Kaye Tsika

Growing in Favor: Daily Devotions for Walking in Blessing with Billie Kaye Tsika

Get Married, Stay Married with Billie Kaye Tsika

Parenting with Purpose with Billie Kaye Tsika

Paul E. Tsika

CREATED FOR MORE

Discovering God's Transforming Grace

 Take note that the name satan and related names are not capitalized. We choose not to acknowledge him, even to the point of violating grammatical rules.

DESTINY IMAGE® PUBLISHERS, INC.
P.O. Box 310, Shippensburg, PA 17257-0310
"Publishing cutting-edge prophetic resources to supernaturally empower the body of Christ"

This book and all other Destiny Image and Destiny Image Fiction books are available at Christian bookstores and distributors worldwide.

For more information on foreign distributors, call 717-532-3040.
Reach us on the Internet: www.destinyimage.com.

ISBN 13 TP: 979-8-8815-0532-5
ISBN 13 eBook: 979-8-8815-0533-2

For Worldwide Distribution, Printed in the U.S.A.
1 2 3 4 5 6 7 8 / 29 28 27 26 25

DEDICATION

I express the deepest gratitude of my heart in this dedication. This Person continues to be the most instrumental Person in my spiritual growth, my anointing to minister and my passionate love for the Lord Jesus. He is always with me, always teaching, always correcting, and always leading me in the paths of righteousness for His name's sake. He brought me up out of a horrible pit and convicted me of my lostness when I was afar off, He opened my heart to the gospel; He introduced me to Jesus as Lord; He baptized me into the body of Christ; He indwells me today as a born-again believer; and, my body is His temple.

He is the Blessed Holy Spirit of God. There is no one like Him. He's co-equal, co-eternal, and co-redemptive with God the Father and God the Son.

I love Him and I'm eternally thankful for His work in me and for me. My intimate relationship with Christ Jesus is because of Him. My knowledge of God's Word is because of Him.

Whatever I do in word or deed to the glory of God the Father is because of Him. The fruit of the Spirit is because of Him.

So, I dedicate this work by acknowledging that without the Holy Spirit of God, I can do nothing that honors the Father and Son.

I read the story years ago about a young man they called "silly Billy." He was asked to explain the Trinity but couldn't.

He simply said, "Silly Billy that is me, three in one and one in three and all I know is one died for me."

Thank You, Holy Spirit of God, thank You.

ACKNOWLEDGMENTS

Destiny Image Publishing Team: Once again our DI team has done an outstanding job with our latest book. Their commitment to excellence, service, and every detail becomes more obvious with each project. Thank you, Destiny Image, for all your support.

Dr. J. Tod Zeiger: Tod is without a doubt one of the most insightful and powerful pastors of my generation. Our collaboration has yielded great fruit to the glory of God. Once again, his contribution to this work is crucial. Thank you, dear friend.

Billie Kaye Tsika: You inspire me, support me, and are always there for me. Every book I write has your fingerprints all over it. This book is no different. You correct all my bad sentence structure and grammar, and that's no small job. Thank you, my precious wife.

Melanie Renee Gay: Renee is our God-sent executive secretary who has been with us for two years, and she is amazing. Daily she helps me stay on track so I can write, reminds me of all my calls, and keeps the office drama-free so I can read, study, and think. Thank you, Renee, for all you do for our ministry and me.

CONTENTS

PREFACE

I came to Christ in the early 1970s. A time of a great outpouring of the fire of God. Revival, conferences, gatherings of believers asking God for the fire of Heaven to fall on the church.

Daily we were meeting and studying the Word of God. We evangelized, prayed, and witnessed with a passion that ignited fires of revival across the nation. Many Christian movements were born in the '70s, men and women of God raised up and powerfully anointed with a burning desire for the Word of God along with a word from God.

Someone has said that those who come to Christ during a time when the fire of God is falling, are different. I'm not certain how true that is, but one thing I do know, it was a different time because we were awakened to the *much more* of God. We heard repeatedly that we were *created for more.* Not more stuff and things of this world, but more stuff and things of the Kingdom of God.

This has always been my message because it's impossible to exhaust the inexhaustible Christ. To plummet the depths of God's love, the riches of His mercy, and the greatest of His grace is the *much more* of the Christian life.

And so, this book is my attempt to whet your spiritual appetite to seek the Lord with all your heart, knowing that you were *Created for More.*

1

YOU WERE CREATED FOR MORE

LIVE BY DESIGN, NOT BY DEFAULT

A man without a purpose is like a ship without a rudder—a waif, a nothing, a no man. Have a purpose in life, and, having it, throw such strength of mind and muscle into your work as God has given you.

—*Thomas Carlyle*[1]

Martha Berry had a dream to start a school for poor children. She had no books, no buildings, and no money. She only had a heart and a dream to help. She went to Henry Ford and asked for a donation. He gave her a dime! She could have been insulted, discouraged, and quit, but she took the dime, bought a packet of seeds, planted, and harvested a crop, sold it, purchased more seeds, and expanded the garden. After her fourth harvest, she made enough money to buy the building. She returned to Mr. Ford, thanked him for his donation, and showed him what his dime had accomplished. He was overwhelmed and immediately donated $1 million, and the Berry School for Children was firmly established. *God calls us to be productive with the potential we have.*[2]

Martha Berry is a perfect example of someone who chose to live by design rather than default.

Life is about choices. You and I are living the sum of the choices we have made up until now. Some have been good, some not so good.

Either way, it's a fact. I travel thousands of miles a year and meet many people. I speak at numerous conferences and fulfill many engagements. I constantly observe people in a large convention venue or a small room. One of the overriding characteristics I have observed is that there are only two distinctive groups of people. I'm not talking about rich or poor, academic achievers or high school dropouts, but those who are either ***living by design*** or ***living by default.***

I am not suggesting that people *living by design* don't have problems or complex circumstances like everyone else, nor do I suggest they don't feel the pressures of life every single day. These people are determined to live their lives "on purpose." They have chosen to live above their circumstances, not under their circumstances. At some point, they determined why they were put on planet Earth and set about fulfilling the Designer's intentionality for their lives.

You know the people I'm talking about, don't you?

- They don't make excuses.
- They make a way.
- They take responsibility.
- They don't blame others.
- They unclutter their lives.
- They don't sweat the small stuff.
- They have a laser focus on the future.
- They are willing to change and grow.
- They are not afraid to determine who has access to them.
- They are not afraid to make decisions even if sometimes they are wrong.
- They have determined that intentional living is the only way to live.

Those *living by default* are different. The word *default* has become very popular in our culture. Years ago, we used the word to describe financial and contractual dealings. In today's world, when you say the word *default*, your mind immediately goes to your laptop or desktop computer. It literally means a predesigned value or setting that has been supplied when something else has not been specified. When talking about software, default describes preset settings, as when you install a program for the first time, it will load the default preferences.

It is sad to say that this "default" group is getting larger. They are easily recognized:

- They are content to go with the flow.
- Why have goals? You will only be disappointed!
- Why strive for excellence when average will do?
- Life happens, so why worry?
- They spend more time planning their vacations than how to build their organizations.
- They are more content to live someone else's dream than have their own.
- Why bother learning when I already know everything I need to know?
- Success is overrated; not everyone can live "on purpose."

The following are two questions I hear most often:

1. Why am I here?
2. Do I have value?

If you ask these questions to different people, you will get many different answers. In answer to these questions, the materialist says, "Life is all about acquiring things." Those who are into only living for themselves would say, "You have to create your purpose in life and get all you can." Rather than the maturing believer who says, "I want to discover God's purpose for my life and give all I can."

I could go on and on, but these statements show that many people genuinely lack purpose. Without a purpose, a person has no direction, which renders that person useless.

A life without purpose is nothing more than living a sub-par existence.

There is a story told in the Bible about a man who was so zealous for his religion that if you disagreed with him, he would kill you. That is what I call a serious man! His name was Saul, a very zealous and religious Jew who persecuted the early church and did everything he could to destroy it. If you had talked to him, he would have told you, "This is my purpose in life." But the One who created him had a better plan, of which Saul was ignorant. One day, while traveling to another city, Saul came face-to-face with the purpose for which God created for him. The encounter was so dramatic that it changed his life forever. Saul, the religious zealot, became Paul the apostle.

A DRIVING FORCE

Not everyone who discovers their purpose in life will have a dramatic and cataclysmic encounter like this man. But the truth is, you need to find the design for which you were created. Being successful and having accomplishments does not necessarily translate into a sense of fulfillment. Many successful people have been dissatisfied with their accomplishments. If money and success were the only guidelines for living your purpose, then why do so many millionaires commit suicide? Accomplishments without a sense of purpose are meaningless. Life without understanding God's design for you leads to disillusionment and emptiness.

Look around you. Everything you see, whether a massive office building, a car, or the watch on your wrist, has a creator. The only time "something" came from "nothing" is when God spoke in Genesis, and "nothing" heard Him and became "something." For years, scientists have taught the Big Bang theory. I do believe in the Big Bang theory—God spoke, and bang, it happened! To say that you are an accident, or a long line of spontaneous generation, is like saying there was an explosion in your garage and out popped a car.

The purpose of something created is the reason it exists or the creator's original intent for making it. The purpose of a thing created cannot be discovered by asking another thing. Only the manufacturer knows why the thing was created.

You don't walk into your kitchen and ask your coffee maker, "Why are you here? What do you do?" If you didn't know the manufacturer designed the coffee maker to brew coffee, you might think it has another purpose. Maybe the coffee maker is here to wash my clothes (a very small load) or to make hot water? That would be silly, wouldn't it? Yes, because the designer intended the coffee maker to brew hot coffee, not wash your clothes.

The word *abuse* is based on two words: *abnormal and use*. You can't use something created unless you know why it exists and what the manufacturer had in mind when he made it. Therefore, when you don't see the purpose of something, you will end up using it abnormally, which is considered abuse.

Think about it for a moment: what is the driving force of your life? What is the purpose that is moving you forward toward a higher level? A higher level might involve a closer family relationship, a stronger person who provides the material needs of others or achieving financial freedom. You may have come to the point where money is only a means to an end for the freedom that financial security brings. Whatever the reason for what you want, only people who live by design go beyond the point of no return.

Without a strong sense of purpose, you will never get to a higher level because the reasons for what you want are so small that just about anything stops you. People who live by design face the same doubts, fears, or feelings of inferiority that come to everyone. The difference is living by design will give you the inner strength to overcome negativity and propel you past your fears.

All of life changes with the knowledge that you're going somewhere. What if someone walked up to you and gave you an all-expenses paid trip to the Bahamas? Everything was included, even the airfare. I dare say you would be in a great mood, wouldn't you? The day's challenges would be steps taken to get closer to your dream vacation. Staying up late and packing would not seem inconvenient; you would be so excited that you couldn't sleep anyway. You set your alarm for 5 a.m. and probably wake up long before the clock goes off. This is a unique morning full of excitement and joy. Why? What's the difference between this day and every other day? The answer is simple. You know you're about to go somewhere fabulous! You are about to embark on an exciting journey!

TAKE CHARGE

Life is not meant to be lived on the treadmill, getting up every day to fulfill obligations and collapsing in bed at night, only to get up the next day and go through the same hopeless, mundane routine. When your life lacks purpose (because you're not sure of your design or why you're put on planet Earth), you will fill your days with diversions to distract you from the inner feeling in your heart. A better way would be to take charge of your life and do something to change it. Living by design brings inner peace and adds value to everyone around you.

You may have heard the poem by Myra Brooks Welch titled "The Touch of the Master's Hand,"[3] which tells of an auctioneer selling off the estate of a wealthy industrialist. My paraphrase follows:

As the auction ended, the tired auctioneer held up a dusty, discolored old violin and asked mockingly, "Who starts the bidding for this? One hundred dollars? No takers? Do I hear seventy-five? Fifty? Twenty-five? Five? How about a dollar?" he implored, and the audience's laughter echoed around the empty walls.

A faint, cracked voice interrupted the laughter. "Excuse me, may I have a moment of your time?"

A bent-over old man shuffled up to the auctioneer and reached for the violin with a thin, pale hand. With his back to the audience, the old man plucked each string and expertly adjusted the tuning pegs. Slowly turning to the audience, he motioned for silence, and then, placing the violin gently under his chin, he began to play.

Lovely, clear notes filled the room, and the audience sat frozen in awe as the old man serenaded them with a heavenly solo. When the solo ended, the old man bowed deeply at the waist and handed the violin to the auctioneer. He then walked slowly out the door, and everyone burst into spontaneous applause.

The smiling auctioneer held up the old violin and shouted above the noisy crowd, "Now, what is the bid for this most extraordinary instrument? One thousand dollars to the man in the top hat. I hear two thousand from the woman in the front, back to the gentleman…three thousand you say? Do I hear four thousand? Four thousand it is. Do I hear five thousand? Five thousand?

"Five thousand going once, going twice…SOLD! This finely crafted violin is of exceptional value, I must say, at five thousand dollars!"

This story paints a vivid picture of the concept of value and how to maximize it. At the story's beginning, the value of the violin is only one dollar. But by the end of the story, that value had jumped to an amazing $5,000! All it took to dramatically increase the value of the nearly worthless violin was for one knowledgeable person to make a few minor adjustments to the strings and then release the violin's fullest potential by playing it with skill and passion. The point is clear. The value of a product like a violin and the value of a person like you and me can increase 1,000 times over with just a little fine-tuning.

We must always be aware of value. It is said that when a man of money meets a man of experience, the man with experience ends up with the money, and the man of money ends up with the experience. One knows the value of money, and now, the other knows the value of experience.

More than one person has said that if they could only win the lottery, they would be fulfilled and able to do everything they wanted. Not true. A quick look on the internet or at television shows reveals that we live in an upside-down world. I am old enough to remember a time when a man felt that if he worked hard enough and smart enough, he could not only provide for his family but also have enough left over to help those in need. The American dream was not that everyone was going to be filthy rich—but that everyone had an equal opportunity to live out the purpose for which they were created. Just because you come into a large sum of money doesn't mean you're going to fulfill your purpose and add value to someone else's life.

Money has no morals. It takes on the value system of the person who has it. If you have no core values without money, you won't change your core values with money! The longer I live, the more I am convinced that *money reveals character; it doesn't create it.*

ARE YOU READY TO LIVE BY DESIGN, NOT BY DEFAULT?

I helped write a mission statement for Worldwide Dream Builders, and in that mission statement, the last phrase says, "God created you for greatness." There can be no greater joy in life than for you to finally and fully realize that.

Let's discuss two important questions that will help redirect your life back to its original design:

QUESTION 1: ARE YOU SICK AND TIRED OF BEING SICK AND TIRED?

Do you ever get a sense that your life is like running on a treadmill? Billie, my wife, and I try to walk or run on our treadmills in our workout room daily because it's very beneficial and will do wonders for our hearts. But the one thing about walking on a treadmill is that the view never changes, no matter how far you walk. In our case, the view is watching Joyce Meyers on TV. Understand me. I'm not saying that exercise is not beneficial. It's an activity that we should all be involved in, and we get as much out of the Word as we do the walk when we're walking. Now that's a mouthful.

My point is this: many people live their lives running as fast as they can, getting nowhere, and the view never changes. When this happens, relationships begin to slip, and once strong commitments weaken, the fire (passion) that once burned brightly in your heart slowly dies. When the fire goes out, the desire that once motivated you takes a backseat, and you spend most of your days thinking about what could have been. It doesn't have to be this way.

QUESTION 2: ARE YOU REALLY LIVING UP TO YOUR FULL POTENTIAL?

I suggest you read and reread my book *Releasing Your Full Potential* at least once a year. Why do I think it's essential for you to read my book on potential? In the book, I discuss how you act with respect to how you see yourself.

Sadly, most people on planet Earth will never discover who they are, while others settle for only a portion of their true potential. We all have the same ability to decide to fully use our gifts, talents, abilities, and capabilities. The question is, will we exercise this option to maximize our potential?

Definition of potential:

- Having or showing the capacity to develop into something in the future.
- Latent qualities or abilities that may be developed and lead to future success or usefulness.
- The possibility of something happening or of someone doing something in the future.

In his book *Understanding Your Potential*, Dr. Myles Munroe describes potential this way: "Potential, the unexposed, untapped, hidden, dormant revelations that lay beneath the accumulated dust and grime of many years. Potential. Strength and beauty that lay unmarred by the ravages of fire, wind, and water. The possibilities of rebuilding after years of destruction, decay, and neglect."[4]

Since writing my book on potential, I've continued to discover more truths about this neglected issue. If you want to reach your full potential, you must face two uncomfortable facts:

Fact 1: Have you settled for the life you have now?

So many people are living far below what God intended for their lives. Settling for average is not what we are called to be, which is why so many people live frustrated lives. Somewhere along their journey, they gave in to their circumstances.

A good example would be from the life of Terah, Abraham's father. God initially told Terah to take his family to the Promised Land. They were on an exciting journey full of hope and excitement. But as you read the biblical story in Genesis chapter 11, you discover that he stopped short of his destination. We don't know all the reasons why he stopped. The definition of his name may give us a clue. Terah means "turning." He turned away from his God-given potential to lead his family in the direction God had given him and settled for far less.

Maybe Terah got tired of the long journey, which was undoubtedly challenging and full of obstacles. Whatever the reason, he did not live up to his full potential. It was much later when God told Abraham to leave his father's house and travel to where God initially told his father to go!

Sometimes we are in danger of settling for less than God intends for us to have. Like Terah, we get halfway there and then quit, never reaching a higher level of living out our potential. Determine never to be content with what is average, minimally acceptable, or "just getting by."

Living up to our potential has one threat that takes on many different faces. The threat is called "satisfaction with where you are." It could take the form of:

- Being endangered by what you have done in the past (successes and failures).
- Settling for less than the best that you could accomplish.
- Choosing what is good over what is great—mediocrity over excellence.
- Allowing fear of change to rob you of the excitement of something new.

American artist James Whistler, who was never known to be bashful about his talent, was once advised that a shipment of blank canvases he had ordered had been lost in the mail. When asked if the canvases were of any great value, Whistler remarked, "Not yet, not yet."[5]

Fact 2: There is more in you than you realize.

Have you ever wondered how God sees you? The next time you look at a forest, consider what you see. You might say, "I see many trees, plants, flowers, animals, and vegetation." That is partially true because what you're seeing is not all you would see—for within each of those things you described are seeds for more trees, plants, flowers, animals, and vegetation. *Created in each is the potential to produce more!* Just by holding one seed of a tree in your hand, you're not just holding a seed but a potential forest. When a seed is planted, the Creator of the universe designs its DNA to produce more than is imaginable.

What's true in the natural world is also true in the spiritual world. God (your Designer) created everything with potential. The "potential principle" that you see in nature is true in you. I like to observe people from all walks of life, especially those we call "street people," and I have wondered what God's original design was for them. One of the greatest tragedies in life is observing wasted potential.

So, I must ask the question. How does the One who created you see you? You don't have to wonder. He views you through the eyes of eternal love and acceptance. He knows where you are, sees your potential, and knows the person He created you to be. His desire is for you to be all He created you to be, which is more than you desire.

The psalmist David describes it this way in Psalm 139:13-18 (NIV):

> *For you created my inmost being; you knit me together in my mother's womb. I praise you because I am fearfully and wonderfully made; your works are wonderful; I know that full well. My frame was not hidden from you when I was made in the secret place, when I was woven together in the depths of the earth. Your eyes saw my unformed body; all the days ordained for me were written in your book before one of them came to be. How precious to me are your thoughts, God! How vast is the sum of them! Were I to count them, they would outnumber the grains of sand— when I awake, I am still with you.*

Read what He said about you:

- You are fearfully and wonderfully made.
- God knows everything about you, including your desires.
- God is the Author and Finisher of your days.

Considering Psalm 139 and reflecting on the promises, it may be a good time to stop and ask a few questions. And you can rest assured when you start asking questions, your Creator promises to give you an answer. He is not afraid of your questions, so please ask. Good questions to start with:

- "What do You want to do in my life?"
- "What do You want to do through my life?"
- "What do You still desire for me to experience?"
- "What possibilities lie within me?"
- "What potential lies before me?"
- "What could I become?"
- "What did You have in mind when You created me?"

FIVE KEY PRINCIPLES ABOUT YOUR POTENTIAL

The Word of God presents five key principles that are vital for understanding our potential:

1. EVERY PERSON HAS POTENTIAL.

No matter how much you may have achieved or how old you are, there's still more God has for you to be and do! Do not settle for less than your best. Two hippies were talking as they looked at the ocean from the deck of the cruise ship. One said, "Man, dig all that water."

The other replied, "Yeah, man, and that's only the surface." Friend, you've only scratched the surface; God sees much more in you.

2. GOD HAS CREATED EVERY PERSON TO BRING HIM GLORY.

How do we accomplish that? By being the person He made us to be. He made us individuals, and we should fulfill His purposes for us on earth.

3. NO ONE CAN REACH HIS OR HER POTENTIAL WITHOUT THE FATHER'S HELP OR APART FROM OUR GOD-GIVEN TALENTS AND GIFTS.

4. NO PERSON CAN REACH HER OR HIS POTENTIAL WITHOUT FACTORING IN THE SPIRITUAL DIMENSION ASSOCIATED WITH POTENTIAL.

God has not only created you with the gifts and talents to do His work on earth, but He also has created you with the desires, dreams, and disposition to become a person with whom He enjoys fellowship and spiritual intimacy. Part of your potential lies in who God made you to be, not only what He created you to do.

5. ONLY GOD KNOWS THE LIMITS OF YOUR POTENTIAL.

It is impossible to know all that God has planned for our lives. You may feel that you have reached the maximum potential in your chosen profession, but until you allow the One who created you to enter your life, you will never know the full range of all He wants to do with you.

If you have never asked the Lord, "What do You want me to be?" Ask Him that question today. Don't rush; be patient and wait until you get an answer. If you have never asked God, "What do You want me to do with my life?" ask Him right now. You may be surprised at His answer. If you're doing what you love, it's a fair assumption the Lord put that desire in your heart. Be open enough to receive His answer.

When would be a good time to start discovering your original design? Some people are always waiting for permission or a personal invitation to start, so here it is ***start now—don't wait!***

CHAPTER 2

LIGHT THE FIRE AGAIN

IT ONLY TAKES A SPARK

Love life, engage in it, give it all you've got. Love it with a passion because life truly does give back, many times over, what you put into it.

—*Maya Angelou*[1]

Author and Pastor Rick Warren observed the following:

> The creative force behind all great art, all great drama, all great music, all great architecture, all great writing is passion. Nothing great is ever accomplished in life without passion. Nothing great is ever sustained in life without passion. Passion is what energizes life. Passion makes the impossible possible. Passion gives you a reason to get up in the morning and say, "I'm going to do something with my life today." Without passion, life becomes boring. It becomes monotonous. It becomes routine. It becomes dull. God created you with the emotions to have passion in your life, and He wants you to live a passionate life.[2]

Passion is required to fulfill your divine purpose. "Passion concerns our heart—the internal fire that motivates and energizes us to fulfill our purpose and do God's will. God is the source of spiritual passion. The Holy Spirit comes to ignite us with holy fire."[3]

According to the Cambridge online dictionary, "passion is an extreme interest in or wish for doing something, such as a hobby or activities, etc.: very powerful feelings."

Passion will either grow or fade away. It never stays the same. Like a fire, it requires attention and nurturing—if left unattended, it will eventually die out. Just as a fire needs fuel, passion must be constantly maintained. If we allow it to burn out, we make room for a silent enemy to creep into our hearts: apathy. Apathy isn't just a mindset, it's a condition that takes root in the heart, and the fire will die before long.

If you're still not sure the world has turned upside down, consider that it is all right in the American culture to be passionate about anything and everything except your faith. All you must do is go to your local bookstore and look around, and you will see books and magazines talking about passion for:

- Hollywood stars
- Sports
- The latest fashions
- Every type of cuisine you can imagine
- Politics
- Fast cars – Old cars – Classic cars
- Travel
- Etc., etc., etc.

For example, there is nothing wrong with football or baseball or any other sport. You can scream your head off so much that you can barely whisper at the end of the day. When your team loses, you can beat your head against the wall. That's okay because you're a fan—an abbreviation for fanatic. Act like a complete fool and those around you will say, "He loves his team." That is perfectly acceptable because, after all, it lights your fire. When your team wins, everything is right in your world.

But heaven forbid that you should become passionate about God. That is something frowned upon in our culture because, after all, people view spirituality only for the insecure and weak-minded. It's okay to cheer for your favorite football team on Saturday (or Sunday), depending on whether you are a college or professional football fan.

In our culture of tepid Christianity, though, don't you dare go to church on Sunday morning with enthusiasm or excitement and let it spill over on Monday morning at work. After all, you must not become too emotional about serving God! Please keep it to yourself. It's a private matter. Don't discuss it. Leave it inside the four walls of the church.

Remember the first line of that little chorus young people sang around the campfire? "It only takes a spark to get a fire going, and soon all those around can warm up to its glowing."[4] We may look back now and think how simplistic those words were. But sometimes we need to remember that it's the simple things that bring the greatest truth.

THREE SPARKS THAT IGNITE A BLAZE

> *Though one may be overpowered, two can defend themselves.* ***A cord of three strands is not quickly broken*** (Ecclesiastes 4:12 NIV).

SPARK 1: TAKE STEPS TO BALANCE YOUR LIFE (LISTEN TO SOLOMON)

> *That's when I called it quits, gave up on anything that could be hoped for on this earth. What's the point of working your fingers to the bone if you hand over what you worked for to someone who never lifted a finger? Smoke, that's what it is. A bad business from start to finish. So what do you get from a life of hard labor? Pain*

> *and grief from dawn to dusk. Never a decent night's rest. Nothing but smoke* (Ecclesiastes 2:20-23 The Message).

Before I share my thoughts on achieving balance, I want to make a brief point. I have always taught that there is no such thing as balance, and in this context, I believe that's true. I emphasize that focus is the key issue because you can't genuinely concentrate and give your full attention when your mind is divided or distracted by other thoughts. However, the concept of balance in this chapter offers more of a 10,000-foot view of life, while the focus I teach deals with the practical details where the "rubber meets the road." However, in life, we need both.

Out of Balance Equals Out of Control

If you want to see a disaster waiting to happen, look at people living their lives out of balance. Consider what has happened to so many famous people who seemingly had it all, only to lose it all when their lives ran off the rails of balance.

- Joe Louis. Though Joe Louis earned more than $4.6 million during his career as a professional boxer, he received only $800,000 as most of the money went to his handlers. Nevertheless, he continued to be generous, taking care of his parents and siblings. Many of the businesses in which he invested failed, and he died in debt.
- Mickey Rooney. Despite earning millions of dollars during his career, he was plagued by financial problems as he gambled away his fortune. In 2005 he described himself as broke. He died in 2014 with his properties valued at $18,000. At the time of his death, he owed taxes and medical bills.
- Sammy Davis Jr. After his death, Sammy Davis Jr. left an estate worth $4 million, but his wife had to auction it as he owed the

Internal Revenue Service around $7 million. His friends from the music industry conducted a concert to raise funds.

- Michael Jackson. The "King of Pop," Michael Jackson, though he sold over 61 million records, died with a debt of $400 million.[5]

Volumes could be written with examples of world-famous people who have self-destructed because they lacked balance.

So I caution: Successful people have time to spend with their families, pursue personal goals, and advance their careers. This balance transcends to those we have meaningful associations with and contributes to their development of a wholesome lifestyle. Read and remember this following statement very carefully: *A balanced lifestyle enables us to not only begin well and live well, but far more importantly, to end well.*

God does not intend for us to be shooting stars or fireworks Christians. He intends for us to succeed in life. This, my friend, requires balance.

One book stands above the rest on how to live a balanced life. It's in every bookstore, and you probably own more than one. It's the BIBLE (Basic Instructions Before Leaving Earth), God's instruction book for every facet of our life, even how to live in balance.

> *You make known to me the path of life; you will fill me with joy in your presence, with eternal pleasures at your right hand* (Psalm 16:11 NIV).

The best example of living a balanced life is found in the life of the most outstanding leader ever: Jesus.

> *And Jesus grew in wisdom and stature, and in favor with God and man* (Luke 2:52 NIV).

This passage refers to Jesus during His young life. This statement is recorded about Jesus soon after returning from His trip to Jerusalem, where His parents' noticed He was missing. His parents found Him at the temple, reasoning with the priests.

We don't see Jesus again in Scriptures until He is a grown man, but what was going on in the meantime? He was growing and maturing and became the model of how to put your life together in proper balance.

The following four characteristics of Jesus's growth are our model for growth. When these areas are in order, we will find a balance that leads to fulfillment.

Four Areas in Life That Need Balance

1. *Mental:* Jesus grew in *wisdom. "Do not be conformed to this world, but be transformed by the renewing of your mind…"* (Romans 12:2 NKJV). Do you want to change the course of your life? Change the way you think.
2. *Physical:* Jesus grew in wisdom and *stature. "For you were bought at a price; therefore glorify God in your body and in your spirit, which are God's"* (1 Corinthians 6:20 NKJV). We need to understand that our bodies are indeed the temple of the Holy Spirit, and there is a connection between how we treat our bodies and the balance of our lives.
3. *Spiritual:* Jesus grew in wisdom, stature, and *favor with God. "Grow in grace and knowledge of our Lord Jesus Christ…"* (2 Peter 3:18 NIV). True spiritual growth comes from finding the balance between the mind and the heart. Spirituality goes beyond just acquiring knowledge; it's about becoming more like Jesus in your mindset and behavior.
4. *Social:* Jesus grew in wisdom, stature, and favor with God *and man.* The definition of *balance* in the Merriam-Webster dictionary is: "When all of the parts are in harmony." We must take inventory to keep our lives in balance. *"The wisdom of the prudent*

is to give thought to their ways, but the folly of fools is deception" (Proverbs 14:8 NIV).

SPARK 2: RELEASE YOUR GIFTING.

An unused gift will cause you to lose your passion for life and your passion for God. First Peter 4:10 in the Contemporary English Version says, *"Each of you has been blessed with one of God's many wonderful gifts to be used in the service of others. So use your gift well."* Remember that God has equipped you with specific talents, abilities, a unique personality, and gifts—all carefully designed by Him. These gifts, however, are not meant solely for your advantage.

Let me get specific. If you are stuck in a career that does not use your talents and gifts to any degree, you will inevitably lose your enthusiasm, zest, and passion for life. I think that's why I love to see people enter their real purpose in life. Although there are challenges, their passion seems to burn those challenges away as they use their gifts and talents.

Life will burn you out if you don't use your gifts and talents. Studies have shown that 70 percent of all Americans are in a job where their abilities are not used or appreciated. That's tragic. God did not give you talents and then say, "Don't use them. Just go make some money." There's something more important than money. That is using what God gave you. God is grieved when He sees you in a job that's not using your talents. He may be thinking, *Why do you think I gave you those talents? To sit on them?* No. If you do that, you're going to lose your passion.

J. Oswald Sanders writes, "The round of pleasure or the amassing of wealth are but vain attempts to escape from the persistent ache.... The millionaire is usually a lonely man, and the comedian is often more unhappy than his audience."[5] That doesn't have to be true; it depends on you and how you approach life.

It's a fact that no job will fully tap into all your talents and gifts, and it's unlikely you'll ever find a career that brings complete fulfillment. Why is that? Because God never intended for a career to be the source of your total satisfaction. Only He can fill that space because your life is about far more than just your profession or calling. God's desire is for you to have a ministry that goes beyond your ambitions—reaching out to impact and invest in the lives of others.

There is a principle that cannot be ignored. God has given everyone specific attributes, characteristics, and talents, and then He says, in essence, *"If you use what you have, I'll increase it, but if you don't use it, you lose it"* (see Mark 4:24-25).

Let me ask you a question. If money did not matter, what would you do with your life? You always have a choice. You can spend your life pursuing power, money, or material things—or you can pursue a life of fulfillment. You will always find the power to be your best in the context of doing your best at what you do best.

When we do what we love, we will love what we do, and we not only get more done, but it's a fact that we do it more efficiently and better. The rewards are enormous when we decide that our life is more than just the sum of what we can "gather." The accumulation of material things will never substitute for the joy, freedom, and delight that comes from simply doing your best with the talents and gifts God has designed for you.

SPARK 3: MAKE SURE YOUR PURPOSE AND DIRECTION IN LIFE ARE CLEAR.

One of the fastest ways to quench your passion and fire is to live without a clear sense of direction and purpose. If you don't know your purpose in life, why bother to get out of bed? Why put forth time and energy into an activity without direction? Maybe you've felt like Isaiah, who says in Isaiah 49:4 (NLT), *"I replied, 'But my work seems so useless! I have spent my strength for nothing and to no purpose.'"*

One thing I've noticed about people who live with a clear direction is that they live according to solid principles. Purpose-driven people face the same external forces we all deal with: self-doubt, time limitations, lack of energy, and constant change. Yet, somehow, they rise above all the difficulties and prevail. What makes them so different? What causes a person to break through and move forward at all costs?

Is it because they are more intelligent than everyone else? Is it because they have a more pleasing personality and a brighter smile? I don't think so. No, people have a resilient spirit because they have come to a place where they know there is a reliable set of principles to live by:

- They know where they came from.
- They know why they are here.
- And they know where they are going.

One of the most important principles is to constantly enlarge your expectations because you are a "magnet." Proverbs 23:7 (NKJV) states: *"As he thinks in his heart, so is he."* In other words, whatever you expect, think about, or focus on will eventually become your experience in life. It's called the principle of "attraction." The principle of attraction is like a magnet, we are attracted "to everything" we receive—both positive and negative.

It takes more than just saying you want to expand your expectations. Just saying you want to do it will not make it happen. The first step is to change your self-talk. I'm sure you've read the same statistic that I have: 80 percent of self-talk is negative.

Our mind is powerful, and it can be our enslaver or our slave. It hears without bias and responds without reference to positive or negative input. If our language is negative, no matter how hard we try to become financially independent, lose weight, stop smoking, or deepen our relationships, we won't succeed. Why? Because our language (self-talk) becomes a co-conspirator of emotional sabotage.

Our subconscious mind is a storehouse of our self-image, and we believe the information it stores is accurate, whether true or not. We must send our minds positive images and pictures, even if they do not represent current reality. That's one reason Billie Kaye always reminds the women to whom she ministers to "Stop *listening* to yourself and start *speaking* to yourself, and what you speak is the Word of God. Ephesians 5:19 (NKJV) says, *'Speaking to yourselves in psalms and hymns and spiritual songs, singing and making melody in your heart to the Lord.'*"

If the results you desire on the outside do not match what you're thinking on the inside, it's time to change the negative blueprint that your mind has created over time. I have heard that what you think is less important than what you do. But what you believe eventually will lead to the reality you create! You will conversely behave consistently with what you believe.

I have a strong sense that the apostle Paul had it right when he says in Philippians 4:8 (NIV), *"Finally, brothers and sisters, whatever is true, whatever is noble, whatever is right, whatever is pure, whatever is lovely, whatever is admirable—if anything is excellent or praiseworthy—think about such things."*

Another critical step to ensure your purpose and direction are clear is to constantly take inventory and reevaluate the principles with which you choose to live your life. What core values and principles are you using as the foundation of your inspiration? Make sure that when you're climbing the ladder of success, it is not leaning against the wrong wall!

Sometimes, we need to slow down to smell the roses and ensure that our activities and energy are based on foundational principles. These principles will move you in the right direction with a clearly defined purpose. Our capacity to receive is determined by what we believe we are worthy of. What we believe we are worthy of is determined by our picture of ourselves. What we see—is what we get!

After changing your self-talk from negative to positive and taking inventory to reevaluate principles, another step will keep your focus in the right direction. It's time to stop verbalizing expectations and start writing them down and keeping them constantly in front of you. Remember, your expectations must be built on the firm foundation of a clear direction and purpose.

For example, over the next 12 months, I expect to:

- Strengthen my family relationships.
- Increase my investment in the lives of others.
- Do everything necessary to increase my mental, emotional, and physical fitness.
- Deepen my relationship with God, thereby strengthening my faith.
- Set my expectations with a laser focus, not allowing silly distractions to dim my vision.
- Determine not to quit no matter how difficult things become.

Your list may be different from this one. Take the time to make your own list and keep it before you. It's not just about setting goals but establishing a clear direction for your goals. Be realistic about your expectations. Someone may say, "Well, I've always wanted to play centerfield for the Atlanta Braves." Now if he's 47 years old, 20 pounds overweight, and only played baseball one year in high school, I would not call that a realistic expectation, would you? That's called living a fantasy! Get real, get serious, and get to work!

> Man is like an onion. His potential is exposed one layer at a time until all he is is known by all.
>
> —Myles Munroe

Nothing matters more than knowing (and living) that we have a clear sense of purpose and direction. God put you on earth to fulfill your purpose, and nothing else can compensate for it: not fame, not wealth, not success, and not pleasure. Nothing can compensate for life without meaning. So, whenever your purpose becomes unclear, you tend to forget why you're here in the first place, perpetuating your loss of passion. Take all necessary steps to keep the fire burning.

What steps will you take to reignite your passion?

1. What would you do now if there were no limits on how far you could go?
2. What steps will you take to fan the flame of spiritual passion?
3. What is your spiritual temperature? Hot______? Cold_____? Lukewarm_____?

Don't make the same mistake Pharaoh made when Moses offered to stop the plagues. Pharaoh added his name to a long list of those who had a choice to change or spend another night with the frogs. It would be fair to say that Pharaoh made a wrong decision and sealed his destiny when he uttered one word, *"Tomorrow."*

Moses told Pharaoh, *"'I leave to you the honor of setting the time for me to pray for you and your officials and your people that you and your houses may be rid of the frogs, except for those that remain in the Nile.' 'Tomorrow,' Pharaoh said. Moses replied, 'It will be as you say, so that you may know there is no one like the Lord our God. The frogs will leave you and your houses, your officials and your people; they will remain only in the Nile'"* (Exodus 8:9-11 NIV).

Another example of this foolish thinking is an incident from the American Revolution that illustrates what tragedy can result from procrastination:

> It is reported that Colonel Rahl, commander of the British troops in Trenton, New Jersey, was playing cards when a courier brought an urgent message stating that General

> George Washington was crossing the Delaware River. Rahl put the letter in his pocket and didn't read it until the game finished. Then, realizing the seriousness of the situation, he hurriedly tried to rally his men to meet the coming attack, but his procrastination was his undoing. He and many of his men were killed, and the rest of the regiment were captured. Nolbert Quayle said, "Only a few minutes' delay cost him his life, his honor, and the liberty of his soldiers. Earth's history is strewn with the wrecks of half-finished plans and unexecuted resolutions. *"Tomorrow" is the excuse of the lazy and refuge of the incompetent.*"[6]

You can't move into tomorrow with yesterday's thinking. When tomorrow arrives, it's renamed today. If you have not prepared for tomorrow, today will look much like yesterday.

FIVE KEYS TO TOMORROW THINKING

1. DON'T TAKE THE PATH OF LEAST RESISTANCE.

Resistance is wrong, uncreative, and judgmental thought that attempts to dominate your thinking. Focus on your thought life because thoughts create perception. Learn to take ownership of your thoughts or it will never become yours.

2. RELEASE YOUR YESTERDAY.

You were not created to carry yesterday and tomorrow at the same time. God gives you today to decide if you want to live in memories or future destiny. Don't allow the pain of yesterday to hinder your thoughts of tomorrow.

3. ENJOY CHANGE. IT'S HERE TO STAY.

Since God never changes, guess who does? Everything and everyone will change, and so will you. The successful ones anticipate and appreciate change. To become a tomorrow thinker, a collection of changes is necessary.

4. SURROUND YOURSELF WITH OTHER TOMORROW THINKERS.

Whatever is around you ultimately shows up within you. Every time God wants to bless you, He will send someone into your life who is a tomorrow thinker.

5. FOLLOW DIVINE INSPIRATION.

Whenever we ask God for a tomorrow, He gives us instructions for today. Our obedience continues the process, while our disobedience delays it. God has birthed this day so you may birth life into your tomorrow. Live today but think tomorrow!

Start now, don't delay any longer, or you will never get started. And whatever you do, don't spend another night with the frogs!

3

TURN YOUR FAILURE INTO SUCCESS

Failures are fingerposts on the road to achievement.

—C.S. Lewis[1]

The Titanic, once seen as a symbol of luxury and invincibility, represented the lavishness and overconfidence of its time, much like the British Empire. People boarded the ship, fully believing it was unsinkable. However, that confidence quickly became complacency when the Titanic hit an iceberg. Captain Smith and his crew had received multiple warnings but failed to slow down or take precautions. There were no proper lifeboat drills, and when disaster struck, the passengers were utterly unprepared, leading to a much larger loss of life than necessary.

Two other ships, the Californian and the Carpathia, played significant roles that night. Though cautious, the captain of the Californian chose to stop his ship because of the ice, but he ignored distress signals from the Titanic and did nothing while watching the tragedy unfold. On the other hand, Captain Rostron of the Carpathia took immediate action. Upon hearing of the Titanic's trouble, he turned his ship around, got his crew ready, and navigated through dangerous ice fields to rescue survivors. His actions showed authentic leadership and bravery.

The sinking of the Titanic reminds us of the dangers of complacency, the need for good leadership, and the importance of being prepared for the unexpected. Whether the loss of a dream or a tragedy, unforeseen challenges often change our lives.

Little did the captain of the Titanic know that something was stalking him that night that would change his life forever. What would it be?

THE REALITY OF FAILURE IS EVER PRESENT

It is a stalker. *It* is mean. *It* is cruel and does not discriminate. *It* will stalk you with an eagle's eye and a lion's cunning. No method is too harsh or inhumane. *It* plays no favorites and has no conscience. Rules of normal behavior do not apply, and *it* doesn't care if you're rich or poor, educated or illiterate, man or woman.

It will haunt you in the middle of the night, whispering in your ear:

- You're not good enough.
- Your time has passed.
- It's time to give up your dream.
- Everyone knows you're a loser.
- You're crazy for thinking that you could ever be successful.
- Your 2- to 5-year plan has turned into 7-to-10 or 12-to-15 years. Now what?
- Your failure has disqualified you.
- You and your spouse are never on the same page.
- Give up, give in, and go back.

The greatest joy of *it* is to watch grown men and women weep over their failures. *It* watches as marriages break apart and entrepreneurial spirits die. *It* is unrelenting and will not stop until all its goals are reached. The ending doesn't matter if the victims never get up and try again. To rob, kill, and destroy are *its* main objectives. A life ruined brings *it* satisfaction.

"What is *it* you ask?" You may have met *it* before and did not recognize the name. *It* may have been introduced as a disappointment, catastrophe, setback, or malfunction. *Its* name? ***Failure!*** Until *it* is confronted and exposed, *it* will continue to exploit and destroy anyone who crosses *its* path.

Denis Waitley observed that "Failure should be our teacher, not our undertaker. Failure is delay, not defeat. It is a temporary detour, not a dead end. Failure is something we can avoid only by saying nothing, doing nothing, and being nothing."[2]

Failure isn't limited to the 21st century. Men and women of every generation have testified that they have been exposed to failure. At the beginning of creation, we know that Adam and Eve endured failure. They had a perfect environment filled with everything their hearts could desire. God called them to make the earth beautiful and fill it with children to enjoy.

It all changed when satan moved into this perfect environment and began tempting Adam and Eve with the idea that they could be as wise as God. "Just eat this, and you will know what you're missing." You know the rest of the story.

Plenty of others named in the Bible failed in some form. I'm not just talking about the bad or the insignificant. God's champions, the chosen and commissioned ones, experienced failure. I'm sure they never dreamed their failures would be recorded and thousands of years later still talked about and laid bare for you and me to read about.

For example:

- Abraham's wife, Sarah, convinced him to have a child by another woman. (Genesis 16)
- Sampson, the strongest man ever, could not control his wild nature, leading to his downfall at the hands of a woman. (Judges 16)
- King David, a courageous warrior, creative musician, and man after the very heart of God, fell victim to uncontrolled desires leading to adultery and murder. (2 Samuel 11)

- Perhaps Solomon, the wisest man in the Old Testament, eventually neglected his time with God and lost the intimacy he once knew. At the end of his life, he was bitter and lonely. (1 Kings 1)
- Elijah, who possessed enough courage to challenge 450 prophets of Baal, was brave enough to confront King Ahab; but the threat of one woman caused him to run for his life. His depression was so great that he wanted to die. (1 Kings 17)

Although the Bible records the failures of many, it also records how these champions rose from the pit of defeat to conquer the enemy called *failure.*

RECENT EXAMPLES

That was another time long ago, what about recent history?

J.K ROWLING

The author of Harry Potter spoke to the graduating class of Harvard in June 2008. She didn't talk about success. *She talked about failures,* her own. I absolutely love her quote: "You might never fail on the scale I did," Rowling said to that privileged audience. "But it is impossible to live without failing at something unless you live so cautiously that you might as well not have lived at all—in which case, you fail by default."[3]

COLONEL SANDERS

The founder of KFC started his dream at 65 years old! He got a social security check for only $105 and was angry. Instead of complaining, he did something about it. He thought restaurant owners would love his fried chicken recipe, use it, sales would increase, and he'd get a percentage of it. He drove around the country knocking on doors, sleeping in his car, and wearing his white suit. Do you know how many times people said no until he got one yes? He was told no 1,009 times![4]

WALT DISNEY

Here was the man who gave us Disney World and Mickey Mouse. His first animation company went bankrupt. He was fired by a news editor because he lacked imagination. Legend has it he was *turned down 302 times* before he got financing for creating Disney World.[5]

VINCENT VAN GOGH

He only sold one painting in his lifetime! Just one to a friend. Despite that, he kept painting and finished more than 800 pieces. Now, everyone wants to buy them, and his most expensive painting is valued at $142.7 million.[6]

MICHAEL JORDAN

He's famous for being cut from his high school basketball team, yet turned out to be one the greatest basketball players of all time. He never let failure deter him. I love this quote of his: "I have missed more than 9,000 shots in my career. I have lost almost 300 games. On 26 occasions, I have been entrusted to take the game winning shot, and I missed. I have failed over and over and over again in my life. And that is why I succeed."[7]

There is no success without failure!

WHAT IS SUCCESS?

Collins English Dictionary says that *success* is "the favorable outcome of something attempted; the attainment of wealth, fame, etc., an action, performance, etc.; that is characterized by success. A person or thing that is successful."

FIRST, THE NEGATIVE.

Success is not the accumulation of wealth.

This is called living by the "Golden Rule." He who has the gold makes the rules! Wealth is not necessarily evil if gained with the right motives and reasons. However, just having a significant portfolio does not guarantee contentment or success. You may be worth $100 million and have just been diagnosed with a horrible disease. I dare say that your money will not buy you peace of mind. John D. Rockefeller was once asked how much money it would take to satisfy him. His reply was astounding: "Just a little bit more." Before Rockefeller passed from this life with a $700 million-plus estate, he wrote a book titled, *A Sense of Incompleteness.* Wow, how revealing that was from a man who's been there.

Success is not a feeling.

If you can "feel" successful, you will be successful. This means that your emotions will tell you whether you are successful or not. If your circumstances are good, then you are happy. The continual search for "happiness" is the primary reason so many people are miserable. If happiness is the goal, then misery is just around the corner. Riding the emotional roller coaster will become an everyday experience for you.

The accumulation of things will not make you successful.

Millions think that more "stuff" is the answer to success. While the Bible tells us that God has given us all things richly to enjoy, "things" will never substitute for what's important.

Success is not striving for power and position.

While many view grabbing power as a success, Robert Ingersoll said, "If you want to know the difference between an orator and a speaker, read the oration of Lincoln at Gettysburg, and then read the speech of Everett at the same place. One came from the heart; the other was born only of the voice. Lincoln's speech will be remembered forever. Everett's, no man will read. It was like plucked flowers. If you want to find out what a man is to the bottom, give him power. Any man can stand adversity—only a great man can stand prosperity. It is the glory of Abraham Lincoln that he never abused power, only on the side of mercy. He was a perfectly honest man. When he had power, he used it in mercy...."[8]

SECOND, A FEW THOUGHTS ON THE POSITIVE SIDE OF SUCCESS.

It's incredible how many people live by the motto, "I'm hoping for the best, yet bracing for the worst." They never give much thought to planning or thinking about where they want to be one month from now, much less have a five-year plan for success. They live with the hope that all things will work out. When the focus is clouded about what kind of life they want, anything that comes along will be fine.

Laurence Shames, writing in *The New York Times,* said John Milton was a failure. In writing *Paradise Lost*, his aim was to "justify the ways of God to men." Inevitably, he fell short and wrote only a monumental poem. Beethoven, whose music was conceived to transcend fate, was a failure, as was Socrates, whose ambition was to make people happy by making them reasonable and just. The surest, noblest way to fail is to set your standards titanically high. The flip side of that proposition also seems true. The surest way to succeed is to keep your striving low.

Many people, by external standards, will be "successes." They will own homes, eat in better restaurants, dress well, and sometimes perform socially helpful work. Yet fewer people are putting themselves on the line, making as much of their minds and talents as possible. Frequently, success is what people settle for when they can't think of something noble enough to be worth failing at.[9]

THE FOUR "WHAT" QUESTIONS

The following "whats" of success will give you a better understanding of God's unique plan for your life.

1. WHAT AM I ON PLANET EARTH TO DO, AND WHY DID GOD DESIGN ME THIS WAY?

You are not an accident or a product of chance. Your Creator ordained you to be born for a specific purpose in your generation. If you never knew your mother or father, or if you were born to parents who were not married, does that make you less of a creation of God? Can anyone decide when, where, and to whom to be born? *No!* You are unique; there has never been anyone like you before, and there will never be anyone like you again. So, cheer up. You were born an original; don't die a carbon copy of someone else's life.

2. WHAT IS MY VISION, AND WHERE AM I GOING?

God has a vision and a plan for your life. He desires to share it with you. The Bible says, *"My people are destroyed for lack of knowledge"* (Hosea

4:6 NKJV). That purpose and vision will serve as a guide to lead and protect you throughout your life.

I cannot imagine Billie and me leaving our ranch in Texas for a city in a state we have never been to without using a road map to find our way. Today, our cars have GPS navigation systems that take you to your destination turn by turn. It would be insane to turn the system off and head in the general direction where we think the city might be located.

But that would be no more insane than for people to live without a clearly defined direction in life. For years in my ministry, I have prayed specifically about our needs. I'm not asking God for general needs but specific needs. I understand God knows before I even ask, but I still pray specifically when I pray for anyone or anything. Specific living leads to specific results, and general living leads to general results. What is your vision, dream, goal, and purpose in life? You don't have to invent one. Start where you are and walk in obedience. Eventually, it will become clearer why God put you here.

> The heart of human excellence often begins to beat when you discover a pursuit that absorbs you, frees you, challenges you, or gives you a sense of meaning, joy, or passion.
>
> —Terry Orlick

3. WHAT IS MY ASSIGNMENT, AND HOW WILL I GET THERE?

Your assignment and specific place in God's master plan is a place only you can fulfill. How will you know? You will know because it will satisfy the deepest longing of your being. The Lord has chosen to endow you with specific gifts, talents, and functions in His infinite wisdom. They are given to guide and assist you to live out your assignment on planet Earth. You have been given natural, intellectual, and supernatural gifts to complete your purpose.

What loving father has ever given a gift to any of his children without being filled with joy at the excitement that child experiences while using that gift for his or her joy and pleasure? If we can do that as mere mortals, certainly the One who created us can in a much greater way. God takes genuine pleasure in watching His children utilize the very gifts and talents that He has breathed into them.

4. WHAT ARE MY CORE VALUES, AND HOW WILL THEY PROTECT ME ON MY SUCCESS JOURNEY?

We will always do what we value most. We will rarely be willing to compromise what we value. When God is the most crucial figure in our lives, fulfillment of purpose will always be at the center of our core values. Why? Our God-given values give us a clear sense of direction for every decision and challenge we face.

When you take the time to answer those four questions, you will be well on your way to understanding the real meaning of success. When you realize that your life is not a series of random events; no matter what comes your way, inner peace and contentment will always take control.

The apostle Paul is a portrait of a man who knew what it was like to face failure. He didn't run or hide from difficulties, he faced them head-on. Paul had already answered the fundamental questions: Why am I here? Where am I going? What is my assignment? Then, his core values guided him in the face of difficult circumstances.

> A story is told about a church that needed a pastor for some time but was having trouble choosing one—not because pastors weren't applying, but because the congregation always seemed to find fault with the pastors. Most pastors were rejected after their resumes were read. Some didn't have enough experience,

some had too much, some did not have enough education, some had too much, and so on.

One day a board member, who was getting very tired of this negativity, decided to do something shocking. The following Sunday he stood up in the pulpit and announced that he had another résumé to share with the congregation. Most of them sat back, folded their arms, and listened, ready to see what faults they could find in the new applicant. The board member began to read the résumé:

"Dear church members, I am writing to apply for a position as your pastor. My experience is more along the lines of an evangelist, but I believe I could fill your position adequately. I've never attended any Bible school per se, but I have a lot of field experience. I don't have a degree on my wall, or a wall for that matter; I've traveled around most of my life renting and doing odd jobs to support myself and preaching wherever I was invited: churches, streets, even jails. As a matter of fact, I've been thrown in jail several times and been involved in a few public squabbles. I've been accused of being anti-Semitic, anti-authority, and causing disturbances almost everywhere I go. But I did have a few conversions to Christianity during my ministry, as well as a few healings. Thank you for considering my application. And I had several men put to death before I became a Christian."

Most people looked up at the deacon with smirks of condemnation, while others chuckled out loud. One man stood up and, still laughing, asked the deacon, "Does this guy expect us to consider him seriously for our pastor? Just what's this fellow's name anyway?"

The deacon replied that the letter was signed, The Apostle Paul! You could have heard a pin drop. (Author unknown)

As you can see, the man who God used to write most of the New Testament would not have been a "fit" for most places today. Would you hire a man with his resume?

A FEW FINAL THOUGHTS

FAILURE CAN HAVE VALUE.

Failure can have value, but only if we do not let the setbacks destroy our lives and allow failure to instead strengthen our character. F.B. Meyer said, "the supreme test of goodness is not in the greater but in the smaller incidents of our character and practice; not what we are when standing in the searchlight of public scrutiny, but when we reach the firelight flicker of our homes; not what we are when some clarion-call rings through the air, summoning us to fight for life and liberty, but our attitude when we are called to sentry-duty in the grey morning when the watch-fire is burning low. It is impossible to be our best at the supreme moment if the character is corroded and eaten into by daily inconsistency, unfaithfulness, and besetting sin"[10]

LAUGHTER IS GOOD MEDICINE.

Give it a try, and you may like it. It's easy to be happy and laugh when things are going great, and difficult when everything goes wrong. Maybe it's time to quit taking yourself so seriously. Learn to look at life like the hockey coach who said, "Last season, we couldn't win at home, and we were losing on the road. My failure as a coach was that I couldn't think of any place else to play."

BE INQUISITIVE.

Never get in the habit of blaming others and asking, "Who." Learn to ask "Why," instead. People who play the blame game never overcome; they just move from crisis to crisis and problem to problem. Our God is large and in charge; "whoops" isn't in His vocabulary. Therefore, remember, when you ask "why," you're not questioning God, you're simply asking Him a question.

FIGHT FOR YOUR VISION AND NEVER GIVE UP.

The aging apostle Paul told a young preacher named Timothy to "Make full proof of your ministry." He told his young protégé Timothy, "Don't quit, don't ever stop pursuing your purpose." Don't let the setbacks set you back, but you push forward toward the "mark of the high calling in Christ" (2 Timothy 4:5; Philippians 3:13-15).

> Success means doing the best we can with what we have. Success is the doing, not the getting—in the trying, not the triumph. Success is a personal standard—reaching for the highest in us—becoming all we can be. If we do our best, we are a success. Success is the maximum utilization of the ability that you have. —Zig Ziglar[11]

I pray you will always remember—failure is never final when you have faith to finish.

So, finish!

4

WHO'S KNOCKING ON YOUR DOOR?

Time is the most precious gift in our possession, for it is the most irrevocable. This is what makes it so disturbing to look back upon the time that we have lost. Time lost is the time when we have not lived a full human life, time unenriched by experience, creative endeavor, enjoyment, and suffering. Time lost is time not filled, time left empty.

—*Dietrich Bonhoeffer*[1]

Access, like purpose and passion, must be protected. The apostle Paul said to his young protégé Timothy, *"Guard the good deposit that was entrusted to you—guard it with the help of the Holy Spirit who lives in us"* (2 Timothy 1:14 NIV).

When you give someone access to your life, you are giving the greatest treasure you can give. Access is giving the right to encounter or exchange with someone, and you hold the keys to that access. Remember, just because you are a believer does not mean that you must allow negative people and influences into your life. While it is true that we are commanded to love everybody, we don't have to allow everybody to influence our lives.

Many years ago, there was a commercial on television about the financial institution E.F. Hutton. When E.F. Hutton spoke, the whole financial world was listening. When the president of the United States gives a speech, it affects not only those who live in the USA but also those who live in the far reaches of the world. Why? As the leader of the free world, his words carry authority and power to change lives. Proverbs 18:21 says that *the tongue has the power of life and death.* What is spoken into your life affects how you think, and how you think affects how you live.

The United States government has an agency called the EPA, which stands for the Environmental Protection Agency. It would be helpful if each of us had our own personal EPA.

Our acrostic for EPA would look something like this:

- **E**xamine - your current environment
- **P**eople - with whom you associate
- **A**ctions - you will take to change an unsuitable environment

Let's look at each word in more depth.

EXAMINE YOUR CURRENT ENVIRONMENT.

God has already given you what you need for success. It's essential to start with what you have, not what you don't have. Where you are, not where you're not. Everyone who is where they are started when they used what they had access to. When evaluating your environment, don't fall into the trap of saying:

- If only I had this.
- If only things were different.
- If only I had more money, then I could do what God wants me to do.

Be careful not to ignore the seeds of success that God has already planted within you. Too often, most people overstate the importance of what they *don't* have as opposed to what they *do* have. God will never ask you to change something like your environment without giving you the necessary tools to accomplish the mission. He wants you to start with what is in your hand.

Overanalyzing your current environment leads to idleness and paralyzes the passion for change. To a double-minded person, everything seems impossible because it seems so difficult. While you may be waiting for extraordinary circumstances to do the necessary things, God is saying to use the ordinary situations already before you to produce extraordinary results.

Your only influence over your future is what you can do in the present. Instead of complaining over what you don't have, be thankful you don't get what you deserve. Most people make the mistake of looking too far ahead for things that are close by. Nothing much will ever be done if you wait until you are ready to change your environment. The Living Bible translation says in Ecclesiastes 11:4, *"If you wait for perfect conditions, you will never get anything done."*

Many items you purchase at the supermarket come with an expiration date. Simply put, the item has a short shelf life. Creative ideas for change also come with an expiration date. As that great showman Arthur Godfrey said, "Even if you're on the right track, you'll get run over if you just sit there." Right now is the most critical moment to decide to change your environment. "I'll do it tomorrow" is the grave marker of opportunity lost.

I read somewhere that wasting time is like slowly giving up on life, not just delaying it! Unfinished tasks and things you haven't even started yet are the biggest causes of stress. Good intentions are like babies crying in church, they must be carried out immediately.

While your past may feel important, it's nothing compared to the amazing possibilities ahead. Let your past be a stepping-stone toward progress, not a place to remain stuck. Stop putting things off or overthinking. You know what you want, so go after it! There's nothing like anticipating a future so bright—it's as if you need sunglasses to face it.

PEOPLE WITH WHOM YOU ASSOCIATE.

God did not design you to fly solo. The correct associations will always bring out the best in you. It's critical for you to recognize with whom you closely associate. Remember, the devil will never use strangers to stop your progress toward your destiny. Wrong associations will always bring out the worst in you, not the best. I am sure you've noticed that when you hang around positive, faith-filled people, you find yourself more excited, less critical, and possessing a clearer vision of the future. After spending time with negative people, you are full of doubt, fear, confusion, and criticism.

A sage man once said, "I can always tell what you like by the friends you keep. You will always attract what you are." I can predict your future by looking at your friends. Where they are is where you're headed. Your friends are a prophecy of your future. If you want to remove negative prophecies from your life, you can do so by eliminating negative people. You will discover that with each new level of assignment and growth, some friends will leave your life, and new ones will enter.

If you want to position yourself to live a more purposeful life, find friends doing what you want to do. Find friends who are going where you want to go; then you can go there together. It's a fantastic concept—you can alter your future by changing your friends.

An old leadership proverb states, "Be with people who will celebrate you and not tolerate you." Each day has 1440 minutes; lack of time is not the problem, but having a sense of direction and using your time wisely are critical factors.

Your success is determined by those you let access those minutes. When you study the secrets of successful people, you discover they control who enjoys access to their time. The greatest treasure you can give someone is access. People who do not respect your time will not respect your wisdom. If you are not careful, you will let wrong priorities and wrong people consume your time.

Paul told Timothy to take the things he had seen and the teachings he had heard and pass them on to a reliable man who would teach others. Listen to his words in 2 Timothy 2:2 (NKJV), *"And the things that you have heard from me among many witnesses, commit these to faithful men who will be able to teach others also."* In other words, only give what I've given you to people who will be producers. Why would you give your time and mentorship to someone who would throw it in the garbage? Access is the only influence that you have in your life. Proverbs 12:26 (NKJV) says, *"The righteous should choose his friends carefully...."* Do not allow anyone access to your time who does not promote your success and is willing to pass that on to others.

Often, people will call me and ask me to help convince their spouse to stay in the marriage. But I have a basic policy. That policy is simply that I do not have five minutes to waste trying to talk someone into staying married. But I have all the time and resources of our ministry to help those who want their marriage to be great. When someone is so uncommitted to something that you must talk them into it, you'll have a lifetime of frustration trying to convince them to stay in the marriage.

THREE TYPES OF PEOPLE TO AVOID

The following are three types of people you should avoid:

1. THE TAKERS (ARE TOXIC).

Takers are people who continually take from the relationship but never give. If people are not adding value to you, lifting you, or

mentor will look beyond being a teacher and will guide us with practical experience to where we need to go. For instance, Timothy had Paul, Elijah guided Elisha, and Joshua learned under Moses.

There are two types of mentors:

First, some do not know you. You listen to their tapes, attend their seminars, read their books, and glean all your knowledge from their experience. I have had many mentors at a distance who have invested in my life who didn't even realize it.

Second, there are mentors whom you do know. One of the most important things you can do with your life is to engage someone you can spend time with who will act as a lighthouse in a stormy sea. This person becomes your beacon who helps when gale-force winds blow you off course. They will be able to recognize your enemy before you do. A trusted mentor can warn you of things to avoid, like landmines that blow you up and detours that take you in the wrong direction.

Mentoring is not something someone does to someone else, it results from a diligent pursuit of another's life and secrets to success. One of the greatest joys I have been afforded is being one of the mentors of many incredible men and women. Billie Kaye and I are blessed to be involved with their growth as we watch them mature. It's similar to the happiness parents feel when they see the children making the right choices and enjoying the fruit of those right choices.

The fastest way to make the right decisions in your work and life comes from the influence and accountability of a mentor.

The apostles had a mentor—His name was Jesus. For three short years, He mentored a handful of disciples, teaching them the most effective way to learn and how to teach those same principles to others. By His example, He showed His followers how to handle angry religious leaders, heal the sick, cast out demons, and feed the hungry.

Today, you find examples of some of the greatest athletes in the world who have mentors, from Olympic gold medalist Michael Johnson to

Michael Jordan. You also discover that some of the most influential leaders of Fortune 500 companies each have one.

2. SEEK A BARNABAS (SOMEONE WHO WILL ENCOURAGE YOU).

In keeping with his name (*son of encouragement*), Barnabas always seemed to be looking for someone to encourage. Without Barnabas, Saul, who later became Paul, would have been lost on the bookshelves of forgotten ministry. Paul, the Tarsus tentmaker, had seemingly been overlooked by the established church and bypassed for meaningful ministry assignments. But Barnabas remembered. Because of Barnabas' influence, the Antioch church found a place for Paul and helped him develop trusted relationships and a respected teaching ministry (Acts 11:26; 13:1-2).

How many men and women have needed a modern-day "son of encouragement" to come alongside and help them get back in the game? Undoubtedly, many were sitting on the sidelines, thrown into the trash dump of uselessness because of a particular failure or some moral breakdown. Instead of encouragement, they find discouragement and a strong sense that their "one shot at success has been lost forever!"

We need to *seek* a Barnabas, but we also need to *be* a Barnabas.

Be a Barnabas:

- To the silent sufferers hidden in the shadows and in the caves.
- To the overlooked and the rejected.
- To those who have failed. Remind them they are not failures.
- To someone who has rejected their calling because they have been told they are now "outside the camp," and their gifts are no longer needed.

Billie Kaye and I have the heart to restore the broken, bruised, and bleeding. We know what it feels like to think no one is in your corner, that no one cares, and that your life is over. We have felt the sting of rejection and the lash of a cruel tongue. We know one word of encouragement is like drinking water in a desert. What we have learned through all our difficult times is simple. When we honestly look at ourselves in the mirror and assign blame to only the person in that mirror and our own choices, we begin to find restoration. God has redemptive people just waiting for broken people to be restored.

One of the problems seems to be that we want to get in God's way before they're ready for restoration. Those who blame, rebel, or are just bitter are not ready to receive restoration. And any attempt will meet with failure and frustration. Godly sorrow and brokenness are always necessary for restoration to be effective. How will you know? You'll know, trust me.

3. TRAIN A TIMOTHY (SOMEONE YOU CAN ADD VALUE TO).

Nothing in life is more satisfying than investing seeds of development into someone else. It has been said that we make a living by what we get, but we make a life by what we give.

Training and investing in someone else may not take you outside of your current circle. Most of us will never travel to a foreign country to train someone (unless God calls us to do so). However, we can open the door for a friend who shows potential, help others discover their purpose in life, or help people in the community.

Entertainer Danny Thomas insisted that "all of us are born for a reason, but all of us don't discover why. Success in life has nothing to do with what you gain in life or accomplish for yourself. It's what you do for others."[3]

It may be that we are training someone to take our place! One of the main goals of leadership is to train others who will be capable and equipped to take over.

ACTIONS YOU MUST TAKE TO CHANGE AN UNSUITABLE ENVIRONMENT.

It's been said that the enemy of great is good. Don't accept good enough as good enough. Tolerating mediocrity only makes you average at best. Unless you are willing to do something beyond what you have already done, you will never grow, and your environment will never change.

It's obvious that nothing happens without action. One of the basic axioms of elementary physics is: "For every action, there is an equal and opposite reaction." The Greek philosopher Sophocles said more than 2,000 years ago, "Heaven never helps the person who will not act." The key to success today is the same as it was 2,000 years ago, and it will be true for the next 2,000 years. Your actions will always speak louder than your words!

PROCRASTINATION

What is the number-one roadblock to action? One word: procrastination.

According to Merriam-Webster, *procrastinate* means "to put off intentionally and habitually: to put off intentionally the doing of something that should be done."

Procrastination is the word a wise man once called *"the natural assassin of opportunity."* Stories are told about the Old West where men were buried up to their necks and left to the elements, predators, and vultures. It was a slow, painful death. Like in the Old West, when we procrastinate, we are experiencing a slow, painful death. That's why I've always called procrastination, "suicide on the installment plan."

I have discovered that most people practice some form of procrastination in their work or family lives. Many have done it for so long that they're convinced it's part of their personality. Dr. Don Carruth, a professor at East Texas State University, disagrees. He says, "Procrastination is simply a bad habit and can be corrected by substituting a good habit—the habit of action."[4]

Take the following procrastination test by answering three questions:

1. HOW LONG DO I TAKE TO ANALYZE A PROBLEM BEFORE I ACT?

I am not suggesting that you rush to a solution to fix a problem. If your track record shows an unusual amount of time spent thinking rather than doing, you are probably infected with the paralysis of analysis. Some people believe that by thinking about something long enough, the problem will magically fix itself. That's one of the reasons for mentors in our lives—to move us into action.

2. HOW FULL IS MY TO-DO-LATER PILE?

If you're looking for ground zero, where projects and assignments die, look in the stack on your desk labeled "do it later."

When Billie and I are driving down the road, and a name comes up, most of the time one of us will say, "I had it on my heart to call that person." And most of the time we will insist that we do it *now.* I heard recently that a dear friend was taken to the hospital. His name was Peter Menk, and he had taken me to play golf at Augusta National. A day or so later he was heavy on my heart, so I called him at the hospital. We had a great conversation and prayed together. The last thing he said was, "Paul, I've really enjoyed our friendship." The next day, he passed. His daughter recently wrote me and talked about the day I called and encouraged him and how much that meant to him. He was a good friend and a godly man. I'm glad I didn't wait; I would have missed saying goodbye to my dear friend.

3. HOW MANY TIMES DO I HANDLE THE SAME THINGS OVER AND OVER?

It's possible that assignments keep coming back like a boomerang because you have been postponing them rather than resolving them. A good principle to follow is to only handle something once and decide what to do with it. I can probably look at your desk and tell you whether you are a "go-getter" or a procrastinator.

THREE KEYS TO A PROPER ENVIRONMENT

1. LEARN TO MANAGE YOUR TIME, OR IT WILL MANAGE YOU.

Time is the great equalizer. Therefore, it is never good enough to say we don't have enough time to accomplish what we need to do. Benjamin Franklin once observed, "To love life is to love time." If time is that important, then why do we waste so much of it?

The only difference between people is what they know. The only distinction between people is how they use their time. You and I have a weapon at our disposal that we can serve, or it can serve us. It's a weapon the wealthy control and hold in the highest value. It's a weapon few discern, many waste, and some even kill. What is it? *Time!* The economies of the world are based on currencies. The currency of life is time. How you value and prioritize time is an indicator of your friendships, finances, and especially your future.

Albert Einstein once remarked, "Time has no independent existence apart from the order of events by which we measure it."[5]

As hard as we try, time is like a rushing tidal wave that demands we deal with it, work with it, and use it. As the old saying goes, "Time waits for no one."

Proverbs 29:18 (NIV) says, *"Where there is no revelation, the people cast off restraint; but blessed is the one who heeds wisdom's instruction."* A lack of vision will always create an atmosphere of chaos. To eliminate the chaos, your vision for order must be clear. Proper order can produce something that creativity does not. Look around; at this very moment, everything you are doing is either increasing order or disorder in your life. God is the God of order; seemingly, the only thing out of order are humans and our use of time. Time management and proper order go hand in hand.

Identifying Sources of Disorder

- **People.** When you allow disorderly people access to your life you are inviting disaster. The one thing they will do is use you as a garbage can to dump all their past problems. Remember, if God has not assigned someone to your life, you're not responsible for helping solve their problems.
- **Places.** An environment of disorder should be avoided at all costs. It may sound simple but disorderly places are for disorderly people. There is no better feeling than to be at the right place at the right time and no worse feeling than being at the wrong place at the wrong time! This may seem trivial, but look around your home and your yard, inside your car, your finances, and the way you keep yourself. These are great indicators of the order or disorder in your life.
- **Practices.** Proverbs 16:25 (NIV) says, *"There is a way that appears to be right, but in the end leads to death."* In other words, you can be sincere about certain things and be sincerely wrong. Lack of knowledge may lead you to places and practices that bring disorder in your life, but you must choose whether to continue or not. You encounter the disorder daily; the question is not whether you will face it but how you respond to it. You must respond and change it before it changes you.

2. IDENTIFY YOUR PERSONAL SOURCES OF INSPIRATION

- Give your attention to information that is uplifting and encouraging.

Thoughts have a presence. When you fill your mind with negativity from the news or the media, that information negatively influences your thoughts. Those thoughts are now a part of your environment. You've taken that negativity from the news, and now you're carrying it with you. That negativity is silently contributing to your actions and to your results.

- Read biographies of successful people.

Success stories can uplift and inspire you to a higher level of growth. In every walk of life, you will find men and women who have overcome obstacles to reach success. Find one who inspires you to overcome your obstacles to fulfill your potential.

- Invest in whatever means necessary to create an atmosphere that ignites your passion.

I have no idea what fuels your energy. It may be a new laptop computer or new furnishings for your office, new wallpaper or simply new lighting. I would not begin to try to figure out what moves you to creativity, but this one thing I know—atmosphere is the key, invest in yourself for success!

3. LEARN THE POWER OF PERSISTENCE

One of the most underrated words in the dictionary is *persistence.* It means consistent daily actions that will lead you to your goals.

Who's knocking on your door? Well, get out of your rocker, fling the door wide open, and you'll find opportunity staring you in the face—TODAY!

So today, I will:

- Determine who will have access to speak into my life.
- Tackle a problem so big that only God can solve it.
- Do at least four things that will stretch me out of my comfort zone.
- Look for someone in need and be the answer to their prayer.
- Make an improvement in some areas concerning my growth.
- Not lose time in the morning and spend all day looking for it!

5

DEVELOP AN EXCELLENT SPIRIT

The nose of the bulldog is slanted backward so he can continue to breathe without letting go.

—*Winston Churchill*[1]

Some years ago, a researcher decided to find out the secret of success. After months of study and countless interviews, he finally gave up. "There is no secret," he said, "It is all related to hard work. One must climb the ladder of success, not just be lifted on an elevator." Thomas Edison astonished those who thought his success was due to luck by stating, "I never did anything worth doing by accident, nor did any of my inventions come by accident." Success often begins at the point where most people would quit. We must believe, then achieve!

T.F. Buxton said, "I hold a doctrine…that with ordinary talent and extraordinary perseverance, all things are attainable." This idea of setting a goal and then relentlessly pursuing it is a formula that has worked for centuries. Even the great dramatist and poet Shakespeare essentially delineated the same success rules. He said, "See first that the design is wise and just: that ascertained, pursue it resolutely; do not for one repulse forego the purpose that you resolved to effect." The wit, Ambrose Bierce, called perseverance, "A lowly virtue whereby mediocrity achieves an inglorious success." Two thousand years ago, Virgil solemnly intoned, "Labor conquers everything."[2]

DEVELOP AN EXCELLENT SPIRIT

To develop an excellent spirit, you must: *maintain a proper perspective, look to the Source of excellence, learn the secret of diligence.* Let's look at each in-depth.

MAINTAIN A PROPER PERSPECTIVE

Perspective means "the interrelation in which a subject or its parts are mentally viewed: point of view—the capacity to view things in their true relations or relative importance, i.e., trying to maintain my perspective."[3]

What does it mean when you think of the term *positive perspective?* Who are the most positive people you know?

- What makes you believe they are positive?
- When you are in their presence, how do you feel?
- What characteristics of positive perspective do you want to have?

The key to developing your potential in performance pursuits and the rest of your life lies in developing your ability to have a laser focus in ways that allow you to develop a positive perspective. Challenges can be faced constructively when you focus on the good things in yourself, your life, and others.

A negative perspective becomes reality when the focus is on finding all the wrong things about yourself, in your life, and in others.

A positive perspective will:

- Concentrate on solutions instead of the problems.
- Look for opportunities, not the obstacles.
- Think the best and not the worst.
- Think success and not failure.

- Learn from upsets and mistakes and turn them into positive opportunities for growth.

Terry Orlick, in his book *In Pursuit of Excellence,* describes a study by Ellis and Harper that identified several *perspectives or beliefs that can interfere* with your capacity to perform to your potential and live a joyful life:

1. The belief that you must always have love and approval from all the people you find significant.
2. The belief that you must always prove to be thoroughly competent, adequate, and achieving.
3. The belief that emotional misery comes from external pressures and that you have little ability to control or change your feelings.
4. The belief that if something seems fearsome or threatening, you must preoccupy yourself with it and make yourself anxious about it.
5. The belief that your past remains all-important and that because something once strongly influenced your life, it must keep determining your feelings and behavior today.[4]

LOOK TO THE SOURCE OF EXCELLENCE

> *O Lord, our Lord, how excellent is Your name in all the earth, who have set Your glory above the heavens!* (Psalm 8:1 NKJV)

The Lord's name is excellent! Throughout the Bible, every person's name describes his character and his identity. God changed Abram's name to Abraham because the "breath of God" was upon him. God changed barren Sarai's name to Sarah, promising her a son. Jesus changed Simon's name to Peter because his life was drastically different. When the Bible declares God's name is excellent, it means what you think it means: God is the most excellent Being, which includes His character, His personality, and all His attributes are excellent!

When God created the heavens and the earth, it was excellent. When God provides salvation for humankind, it is excellent. As children of God, we are commanded to be imitators of God (Ephesians 5:1). We are to follow Him as much as possible, which means we are to be people of excellence—everything we say and do should be done with an excellent spirit.

> *Let them praise the name of the Lord: for his name alone is excellent; his glory is above the earth and heaven* (Psalm 148:13 KJV).

It is past time that Christian leaders fight for excellence in everything we do and speak. For that to happen, our walk and our talk must match, or else those around us will know that we are no different from the world system. As a dear pastor friend said years ago, "Either walk your talk or zip your lip." Great advice for all of us to remember, because we are the only Bible some people may ever read.

Since His name is excellent, and we are people called by His name, we should be excellent people, shining as a bright light in a dark world. The world system is opposed to excellence and will often compromise and take the path of least resistance. Most politicians are elected to office not because of character but because they are willing to compromise and choose power over principles. Too many laws are passed to legalize what God calls sin. The standard approach is, "If we can't handle or justify it, we pass a law and legalize it." Compromise is comfortable, and we look for reasons not to fight for excellence. This attitude has infected the world system and many churches and Christian leaders. It's never easy to raise the standard of excellence.

What is your level of excellence, right now, today?

- Do you pray and listen to the voice of the Holy Spirit who lives within you? Or do you do your own thing and ask God to bless it?

- Are you fighting for prosperity so that you might be a blessing to others? Or do you live with a "just get by" mentality?
- Do you fight to serve others? Or are you just looking out for number one?
- Are you building Christ-centered relationships? Or are you building friendships to promote your agenda?

LEARN THE SECRET OF DILIGENCE

In any challenge we face, any goal we pursue, we can experience a wide range of outcomes: incredible, great, good, poor, or catastrophic. If you study the lives of some of history's most successful people, you will discover that they have experienced the same range of outcomes in one or more areas of their lives. They learned the secret of one skill that propelled them into the stratosphere of success. This powerful tool enabled them to reach impossible dreams.

To name a few:

- George Washington
- Benjamin Franklin
- Clara Barton
- Sandra Day O'Connor
- Condoleezza Rice
- John D. Rockefeller
- Sam Walton
- Walt Disney
- Bill Gates

Diligence is a skill that is learned, not imparted. It can be easily acquired by anyone, regardless of their level of education, financial resources, or intelligence.

Solomon, the wisest and richest man who ever lived, said this about diligence, *"Do you see a man diligent and skillful in his business? He will stand before kings…"* (Proverbs 22:29 AMPC). Although persistence is part of diligence, the most accurate description is in the word *hard-working*. Or, as someone said, not hard-working but "smart working." For example, what tools would I use if I wanted to build an addition to my house? I could take a weed eater, a lawnmower, and a sledgehammer and go to work. I could work for days and consider it "hard-working," but that would not be diligence. On the other hand, if I took the proper tools for building an addition to my house, I could accomplish the work in a fraction of the time, and I would not be working nearly as hard, but I'd be working a lot smarter.

In his book *The Richest Man Who Ever Lived,* Stephen Scott observed the following: "Diligence is a learnable skill that combines creative persistence with a smart working effort rightly planned and rightly performed in a timely, efficient, and effective manner to attain a pure and of the highest quality of excellence."[5]

Solomon outlines five rewards of diligence:

1. If you want an advantage, then you must practice diligence, which will always give you an advantage. *"The plans of the diligent lead surely to advantage…"* (Proverbs 21:5 NASB1995).
2. If you want to rise above your circumstances, learn to practice diligence. *"The hand of the diligent will rule, but the slack hand will be put to forced labor"* (Proverbs 12:24 NASB1995).
3. Diligence leads to fulfillment and contentment. *"The soul of the diligent is made fat"* (Proverbs 13:4 NASB1995).
4. Diligence is a gateway into another realm of influence. *"Do you see a man diligent in his business? He will stand before kings…"* (Proverbs 22:29 AMPC).

5. Diligence will produce increasing wealth and success. *"Wealth gained by dishonesty will be diminished, but he who gathers by labor will increase"* (Proverbs 13:11 NKJV).

PROFILE OF AN EXCELLENT SPIRIT: CONSIDER DANIEL

> *Inasmuch as an excellent spirit, knowledge, understanding, interpreting dreams, solving riddles, and explaining enigmas were found in this Daniel, whom the king named Belteshazzar, now let Daniel be called, and he will give the interpretation* (Daniel 5:12 NKJV).

As a young boy, Daniel had been captured by King Nebuchadnezzar of Babylon. Along with all the other young, healthy, bright men of Israel, he was taken to the great city of Babylon. The city of Babylon was excellent in every imaginable way. The "Hanging Gardens" of Babylon are still known as one of the Seven Wonders of the World. It must've been a daunting sight for these young teenage boys to see the magnificence and the opulence of such a grand city. Nebuchadnezzar, the supreme ruler, had wealth beyond imagination and conquered all other great societies worldwide.

Bible scholars tell us that Daniel was probably between 18 and 25 when he was brought to the center of architecture, wealth, and knowledge of his day. The king had a plan. He intended to take these young Hebrew captives, give them the best food and education, and build the wisest and strongest young men possible to lead his nation.

Daniel had a different plan:

> *But Daniel purposed in his heart that he would not defile himself with the portion of the king's delicacies, nor with the wine which*

> *he drank; therefore he requested of the chief of the eunuchs that he might not defile himself. Now God had brought Daniel into the favor and goodwill of the chief of the eunuchs. And the chief of the eunuchs said to Daniel, "I fear my lord the king, who has appointed your food and drink. For why should he see your faces looking worse than the young men who are your age? Then you would endanger my head before the king"* (Daniel 1:8-10 NKJV).

Daniel could have said, "I am far away from home; no one will ever know if I participate." He could have rationalized his actions in many ways, but he purposed in his heart not to defile himself with their lifestyle.

Daniel's promotion came because the king of Babylon faced a problem. He was greatly troubled and confused by a vision he had seen of a man's handwriting on the wall. The queen mentioned Daniel, who had been appointed by the king's father years earlier as a master of the wise men. She told the king to bring Daniel so he could interpret the meaning of the vision. Daniel already had a reputation for being a man of insight into spiritual things.

FIVE KEYS TO AN EXCELLENT SPIRIT

Daniel had an excellent spirit. His mind, the spirit of his life, and his manner of living were all excellent. How did Daniel develop an excellent spirit? Daniel unlocks the answer to that question with five keys to an excellent spirit:

KEY 1: DANIEL HAD A PURPOSE.

You could say that Daniel had a heart. If you have ever been in the presence of someone who dared to overcome obstacles and not follow the crowd, you might say they have "guts." This simply means they are not easily swayed. Their drive, desire, and motivation keep them from peer pressure, influencing them to do things contrary to their core values. Being different and unafraid to fight for what's right is part of their character.

Daniel was surrounded by compromise and mediocrity but decided to discipline himself and not get caught up in the city's atmosphere. Daniel lived by the motto, *"If 1,000 people say something isn't wrong, it's still wrong."* Truth is never at the mercy of the consensus of what's right. Majority rule is not always correct. Usually, those who don't have dreams or purpose in their heart are the ones who want to take a vote. Making a group decision is easy, and hiding in a crowd is a common characteristic of those who "go with the flow." God doesn't govern by the majority—He alone is the majority. His vote is the only one that counts!

An excellent spirit is not afraid to be different, to stand out in a crowd. There should be something different about Christians. After all, 1 Peter 2:9 (KJV) tells us, *"Ye are a chosen generation, a royal priesthood, an holy nation, a peculiar people; that ye should shew forth the praises of him who hath called you out of the darkness into his marvellous light."*

One of the greatest compliments anybody can give you is to say that you're different and they want what you have.

KEY 2: DANIEL PRACTICED SELF-DISCIPLINE.

It's a fact that if we cannot discipline ourselves, we will never have an excellent spirit. Self-discipline should affect every area of our lives, including the physical, spiritual, mental, and financial.

Discipline and disciple come from the same root word. Excitement and passion will get you out of the starting blocks, but self-discipline will keep you running in the race. Not the ones with the most talent or skills cross the finish line first. It's those who have learned the secret of a self-disciplined lifestyle. You may have all the talent in the world, but you won't last without self-discipline.

A common denominator of self-discipline is learning more than talking. The actual test lies in action; no one has ever stumbled into greatness while lying on the couch. Words without action are the assassins of self-discipline.

Self-discipline and personal growth go together. Just like our attitude, self-discipline is a choice. If you want to get something out of life, you must put something into it.

Daniel demonstrated self-discipline in more than just one or two areas of his life. Those disciplined in small things tend to be disciplined in significant things, whereas those undisciplined tend to be that way in almost every area of their lives.

Self-discipline is necessary to:

- Promote a healthy lifestyle.
- Maintain and organize study habits for personal growth.
- Create extra time in a busy family schedule.
- Create productive time to pursue your dream.

Some may think self-discipline is too time-consuming, rigorous, and not worth the effort. However, self-discipline produces more quality time for the critical issues of life. Plus, what better way for a leader to model the life of Christ than through self-discipline?

Daniel, Shadrach, Meshach, and Abed-Nego were selected for special training. Their decision to refrain from eating the king's delicacies was already determined. Self-discipline is made easier when the decision is made beforehand, not under pressure. They knew what they would not do, so when pressure was applied, they did not crack under the strain. Self-discipline works best when the decisions are made ahead of time and lived according to those decisions.

KEY 3: DANIEL REFUSED TO TAKE SHORTCUTS.

There are some proper shortcuts we can take. We can learn from other people's mistakes and successes. As the old saying goes, *"Don't try to reinvent the wheel."*

What I am talking about is shortcut thinking and shortcut living. It's the attitude of just doing enough to get by. Every farmer knows it takes hard work to produce a harvest. It takes patience to sow and hard work to gather. Planting seeds and harvesting are two seasons that require diligence combined with long hours of hard work. No self-respecting farmer would ever consider taking shortcuts.

Shortcuts can be deadly.

Take Jim Madsen on Yosemite's El Capitan in 1968. A veteran and skilled climber, he rappelled from the top of El Capitan to rescue some friends. In his haste to reach them, he apparently neglected to check his rope—it wasn't knotted at the end, and he rappelled right off the end, falling 2,500 feet to his death. In his hurry, he also did not take the time to establish a belay, which would have prevented his fall. Taking shortcuts can lead to trouble. Cutting corners can kill you.[6]

Shortcuts can kill authenticity.

Pastor Henry L. Allen spoke on the dangers of religion and said:

> For many centuries, genuine pearls commanded a high price because of their scarcity. Great quantities of oysters had to be examined before a few that contained the coveted treasures could be found. Then suddenly, the market became flooded with them. After some investigation, the mystery of the abundant supply was revealed. Enterprising individuals had discovered that if a foreign object is lodged in an oyster's tender flesh, the oyster would form a glistening Pearl around

the source of discomfort. Deciding to help nature along, these people artificially induced the process by inserting irritants such as tiny beads and buckshot into the shells. When the pearls had formed, they were carefully harvested. Well, the patrons became suspicious. It was demanded that the new pearls be subject to a special test to determine their authenticity. Although outwardly, they seemed perfect, the x-ray showed their impurity. They had "false hearts" of land or glass. The scam was revealed by looking on the inside![7]

Shortcut thinking will kill creativity.

Shortcut thinking will always choose what's easy instead of what's best. It will choose what's acceptable instead of what's excellent. It will focus on getting by in the short term instead of a willingness to work hard for long-term success.

Where are you deciding to take a shortcut? Remember, shortcuts can be deadly. So, think long and hard before making a career decision, choosing a life partner, entering a new relationship, or making a financial decision that will change your future. One of the things I appreciate most about many of the leaders I work with is their unwillingness to take shortcuts with those they lead to advance themselves. They insist from the people they lead that they build solid parameters for their businesses. This may take a little longer, but these parameters will give them the very best opportunity in the long run for a successful business.

KEY 4: DANIEL DEMONSTRATED HUMILITY.

Now God had brought Daniel into the favor and goodwill of the chief of the eunuchs (Daniel 1:9 NKJV).

These young men were under the care of the chief of the eunuchs. The king had given him free rein to train and be responsible for their assimilation into the ways of the kingdom. Daniel refused to show a rebellious attitude and did not allow bitterness and hatred between them. No doubt had he taken the rebellious approach, he would've opened himself up for a different outcome.

Quite the contrary, Daniel took the approach of loving this man and building a relationship with him. Because of this, God could work through Daniel and create a bond between Daniel and his captor. An excellent spirit refuses a judgmental attitude and a display of righteous indignation. An excellent spirit builds relationships with love, even with enemies.

Daniel's humility gave strength to his words. In his book *The Pursuit of God,* the late A.W. Tozer wrote:

> The humble man is not a human mouse, suffering a sense of his own inferiority. In his moral life, he may be as bold as a lion and as strong as Samson, but he doesn't fool himself about himself. He has accepted God's estimate about his own life. He knows he is as weak and as helpless as God has declared him to be. Paradoxically, he relies on the confidence in the sight of God; he is more important than the Angels. In himself, he is nothing; in God, he is everything. That's his motivating motto.[8]

Because of Daniel's attitude, there came a point when the door of opportunity opened, and he walked through it. King Nebuchadnezzar had a troubling dream, and he was distraught. The Bible says he woke up troubled and in a cold sweat (Daniel 2:1). The king knew that dreams meant something and were considered very important. All the king's magicians and astronomers could not interpret the dream or even help the king remember what the dream was about. They complained that his request was impossible; no one could do what the king had asked them to do.

The king was so upset with the wisest men of his kingdom that he issued a decree of death! Daniel was included with the rest of the wise men, so, he was in a precarious position. How would Daniel respond?

Daniel 2:15-19 (NIV) says:

> *He asked the king's officer, "Why did the king issue such a harsh decree?" Arioch then explained the matter to Daniel. At this, Daniel went in to the king and asked for time, so that he might interpret the dream for him. Then Daniel returned to his house and explained the matter to his friends Hananiah, Mishael and Azariah. He urged them to plead for mercy from the God of heaven concerning this mystery, so that he and his friends might not be executed with the rest of the wise men of Babylon. During the night the mystery was revealed to Daniel in a vision. Then Daniel praised the God of heaven.*

Daniel followed his faith and trusted that God would provide the answer when he appeared before the king again. Faith believes God will work even when the answer is not readily available.

KEY 5: DANIEL KNEW GOD WAS HIS SOURCE.

While it's true that Daniel consulted with his close companions, he knew that God Himself was the ultimate Source of wisdom. An excellent spirit will recognize that having wise friends is essential, but having access to God's wisdom is imperative. Daniel was utterly confident in his ability to tell the meaning of the king's dream. Daniel told the king that no man could answer his questions or interpret his dream, realizing that only God in Heaven could accomplish what could not be done naturally.

> *Daniel replied, "No wise man, enchanter, magician or diviner can explain to the king the mystery he has asked about, but there is a God in heaven who reveals mysteries…"* (Daniel 2:27-28 NIV).

In every circumstance Daniel faced, including the den of lions, he remained consistent and would always:

- Be a man who lives with purpose.
- Practice self-discipline.
- Refuse to take shortcuts.
- Demonstrate humility.
- Recognize God as his Source.

Developing an excellent spirit is a choice, and Daniel chose his daily routine over time. The Bible declares that he was a man of excellence and an excellent spirit. To demonstrate excellence externally, there must first be a development of an excellent spirit internally. Excellence starts on the inside before it's ever seen on the outside. Knowing God makes us humble; knowing ourselves will keep us humble. People look at the outward, but God looks at the heart; therefore, humble yourself under the mighty hand of God so that He may lift you up to a place of leadership in His time.

Excellence is contagious—start an epidemic!

6

HOW HIGH WILL YOU BOUNCE?

There are three ways that men get what they want: by planning, working, and praying.

—US Army General George S. Patton[1]

For some people, success is the ingredient that fuels greater and greater success. For others, it is a narcotic that dulls further action. No leader who rests on their laurels remains a leader for very long.

As stated in the previous chapter, failure is not final unless you allow it to be. You may wonder why I'm spending so much time on this issue. The answer is simple. To defeat a relentless enemy, you must know his tactics and be more ruthless. While I can never exhaust this issue, I hope I can put a muffler on it. Get the pun, "exhaust, muffler." It's corny but true.

Everyone fails. That doesn't mean you must identify yourself as a failure. Failure applies to a situation or a particular time and place. Failure can be an opportunity for learning, recovery, character creation and demonstration if you don't let it devastate you. No commanding general expects to win every battle. Each learns to take his losses, learn from them if possible, and move on. The same is true in any enterprise involving risk. You cannot always avoid failure, but you can refuse to be pinned down by it.

As legendary World War II General George Patton observed, "There is no place to go but down when you are on top. True success is character, and character is measured by how high you bounce when you are toppled from that height and hit bottom."[2]

As General Patton said, success is measured by what you do after you hit bottom. We are living in a generation where everyone has a definition of what to do after you crash to the bottom. Whoever is the "flavor of the month" and sells the most books is the expert. With changing times and changing challenges, we get changing definitions!

How high did the apostle Paul "bounce" when knocked down? Let him tell you in his own words:

> *Now I want you to know, brothers and sisters, that what has happened to me has actually served to advance the gospel. As a result, it has become clear throughout the whole palace guard and to everyone else that I am in chains for Christ. And because of my chains, most of the brothers and sisters have become confident in the Lord and dare all the more to proclaim the gospel without fear.*
>
> *It is true that some preach Christ out of envy and rivalry, but others out of goodwill. The latter do so out of love, knowing that I am put here for the defense of the gospel. The former preach Christ out of selfish ambition, not sincerely, supposing that they can stir up trouble for me while I am in chains. But what does it matter? The important thing is that in every way, whether from false motives or true, Christ is preached. And because of this I rejoice. Yes, and I will continue to rejoice* (Philippians 1:12-18 NIV).

Look at how Paul faced the difficult circumstances. Everything about his experience spelled "failure," but he turned them into "success." How? Let's consider each of Paul's four reactions.

1. PAUL WAS REALISTIC ABOUT HIS SITUATION.

(Philippians 1:12, *"to advance the gospel.")* He faced the possibility of failure head-on and turned it around. He *focused on his desire to spread the gospel—not on his potential failure!* If you spend all your time and energy worrying about not failing, you will increase your chances of doing what you don't want to do. Stop worrying about what is out of your control. Others were adding affliction to his chains, but Paul rejoiced that Christ was being preached!

2. PAUL KNEW OTHERS WOULD BENEFIT.

(Philippians 1:13-14, "*As a result, it has become clear throughout the whole palace guard and to everyone else that I am in chains for Christ. And because of my chains, most of the brothers and sisters have become confident in the Lord and dare all the more to proclaim the gospel without fear.*") He knew his situation was hard and dangerous, but he only cared about others. He kept his eyes off himself and realized many in the palace were being saved.

3. PAUL KEPT MOVING FORWARD.

(Philippians 1:18, *"But what does it matter? The important thing is that in every way, whether from false motives or true, Christ is preached.")* Paul viewed his circumstance as a fresh opportunity, not his final obituary. By our standards, Paul was in line to receive the "failure of the year" award. But in each case, he welcomed failure as an opportunity to keep moving. When shipwrecked in Malta, he ministered to the people. When arrested, he saw it as an opportunity to preach the gospel in jail. He never stopped. His failures were stepping-stones, not stumbling blocks!

4. PAUL STAYED POSITIVE AND KEPT PRAISING.

(Philippians 1:18, *"And because of this I rejoice. Yes, and I will continue to rejoice."*) When our attitudes are right, failure helps us mature. It becomes our teacher, a chance to show us where we have fallen short and an opportunity to change. For most, the *"what does it matter"* of life is an open door to complaining. But Paul would have none of that!

THE ROOTS OF FAILURE MUST BE EXPOSED

If you haven't experienced failure yet, you just haven't lived long enough. Maybe you live in a cave or a deserted island. Even then, I can guarantee something will go wrong!

As we've already discussed, anyone who dares to take risks must be willing to fail. Another lesson I've learned is that some people face failure just because of "life." Yes, it just happens. It rains on the just and unjust alike. It could be because of a downturn in the economy, dealing with a rebellious teenager, or events out of your control. The list is endless.

BUT...

Some people are so busy trying not to fail that they fail by sabotaging their success by offering excuses as to "why something won't work." It's much easier to provide an excuse than to pick yourself up and try again. While you're saying something can't be done, somebody's doing it. One of the great irritations of my life is people who bellyache, gripe, and complain but never offer any solutions. I'd just as soon you keep your mouth shut, please, until you have something intelligent to contribute. As a pastor, I know I should be kinder, but I'll get there. Pray for me.

Making an excuse is simply a way of placing the blame for an internal problem on an external condition. It's a way of looking for a cause that can only be found within. The roots are there, so they must be exposed and pulled up. There's a Yiddish proverb that says, "The girl who can't dance says the band can't play."[3]

We need to learn to turn all our excuses into ex-uses of our excuses, leaving out the "c" for cause.

You have the same assets that all the greats have had. There is no excuse for not using the brain God gave you to accomplish anything you can dream. One of my mentors taught me that if you can imagine it, God can do it. Unfortunately, many have decided to use their God-given talent and potential to think of all the excuses because nothing changes in their life.

If you are living out the definition of "insanity," which means "doing the same things over and over again, expecting a different result," it's time to stop it! Nothing is holding you back if you decide to make it happen!

FOUR EXCUSES THAT PREVENT YOU FROM SUCCEEDING

1. MY TIME IS LIMITED.

How many times have I heard, "I don't have enough time"? It's the go-to excuse. The apostle Paul said, *"Redeeming the time, because the days are evil"* (Ephesians 5:16 NKJV). This may shock your system, but God is not making any more time. You have the same time as the apostle Paul, Albert Einstein, Thomas Edison, and the neighbor who lives next door. The point is, we all have the same amount. The question is, what are you doing with your time? Whether you're a pauper or a king, you have 24 hours daily.

Is it possible that you:

- Have your priorities backward?
- Have splintered your focus?
- Have drained your passion?
- Have a lack of direction?
- Have a severe lack of discipline?
- Don't understand stewardship of your time?

You may be thinking that your time is limited. The issue is the lack of something, but indeed, it is not time. If I could spend one week with you, I could tell you what you value most in life. How is that possible? You will always invest your time in what you think is valuable. For example, if you spend 40 hours a week on your job, you have value in your work. If you value watching television more than spending time with your family, you are again showing where your priorities are.

You will always make time for what you consider important. If you say you need to lose weight yet spend more time staring at a computer late at night, once again, what you value equals your time. Time is the currency that shows what you value. If you're not giving something time, you don't value it. Plain and simple.

Last time I checked, there were 24 hours in a day. If you work 8 hours and only require 8 hours of sleep, what are you doing with the other 8? I have spent my life, whether in the Marine Corps, selling insurance, or in the ministry, trying to use those 8 hours doing the "and then some." I have tried to teach my children and grandchildren that doing the "and then some" is the key to success in any endeavor in life. You do what's required, "and then some." You serve people "and then some." You pray, give, love, forgive, bless "and then some." I promise you those people will have written on their headstones, "They did all they could AND THEN SOME!"

Success in life takes time. You have it; what will you do with it? Your destiny is being shaped and developed in your daily routine. Someone once said a successful routine is the result of right repeated actions.

> Men rarely choose their future; they simply choose their habits, and their habits decide their future.
>
> —Dr. Paul Crites[4]

2. I NEVER SEEM TO HAVE ENOUGH MONEY TO DO WHAT I WANT.

Another classic excuse, "I don't have enough money!" This one is truly an excuse. It embodies the very essence of why some people will never fulfill their dreams.

Who are the rich today but the poor of yesterday? You don't need money to succeed. You need determination and an unrelenting attitude! With these characteristics, you will gather all the necessary funds to start. Make tenacity your friend.

Todd Duncan's book, *The Power to Be Your Best,* tells the story of the great college basketball coach Jim Valvano:

> Jim Valvano was one of a kind. Valvano was the choirboy who hid the matches and would shake your hand and then hand you your watch. By his own admission, he was a rogue and thrived on it. An honest con, one reporter said lovingly. Valvano once agreed to wear a microphone during the game for a feature that was going to run on the six o'clock news. The sports editor later said there was so much material; he could have composed

a sitcom from the outtakes of this colorful coach from North Carolina State. Valvano, in one of the most inspirational speeches of all time given just a few months before he died of brain cancer, looked his team in the face and said, "Guys, never, ever give up!"

There is no better speech to give yourself, especially when those words will have the power to keep you on the right track toward your dreams. Remembering that your life's purpose is to live a life of purpose regardless of how little you have now is helpful. Never allow money to be the master of your destiny. You can always find a way to get something when you're determined to have it. When people say, I don't have enough money, what they are really saying is they don't want it badly enough. They're also saying they don't prize it enough. It's not that important. They want it to be given to them. Money is never the issue, the issue is opportunity, and God has given everyone plenty of that. An issue of the Wall Street Journal had an article years ago that caught my attention. The article simply said, "No one lacks time or money; all they really lack is management." How true that statement is, and I pray it will ring loudly in the ears of today's excuse-makers.[5]

3. I DON'T HAVE A COLLEGE EDUCATION.

This is a classic example of an excuse for being as good as another.

- Walt Disney dropped out of high school.
- Thomas Edison, the inventor of the everyday light bulb, had to join the railroad at 12 years old after receiving most of his education from homeschooling.
- Billionaire S. Daniel Abraham, who founded Slim-Fast, did not have a college education.

- Tom Anderson, who cofounded Myspace, dropped out of high school.
- Dustin Moskovitz is the cofounder of Facebook and a college dropout.
- Jimmy Dean is the founder of Jimmy Dean Foods and a high school dropout.[6]

I would never categorize myself with such successful people. However, God has taken a nobody from nowhere who encountered someone (Jesus) from everywhere and has given Billie Kaye and me a ministry that has touched thousands of lives. This was far beyond our wildest dreams—and all without college or seminary.

4. IGNORANCE.

Ignorance—what an excuse! If you haven't learned, of course you don't know how! This may very well be the worst of the four excuses. Most people want to succeed; they don't know how. They've tried this and that, but nothing seems to work. They eventually give up, resigning to live a life of mediocrity.

To be ignorant means you don't know how to succeed. It means you haven't discovered the system that guarantees your success. In other words, you've not identified the two or three daily tasks that ensure you will succeed. When you're ignorant, you know where you want to go, but you don't know how to get there.

In his book *Outliers,* Malcolm Gladwell repeatedly talks about the "10,000-Hour Rule," about which he states:

> The key to success in any field is largely a matter of practicing a specific task for a total of around 10,000 hours. As an example, he brings up that The Beatles performed live in Hamburg, Germany alone, over 1,200 times from 1960 to 1964, amassing

> more than 10,000 hours of playing time. He also points out that Bill Gates met the 10,000-Hour Rule when, at the age of 13, he spent some 10,000 hours or more learning programming on a high school computer that he managed to gain access to. Give yourself to devote 10,000 hours to any field, and you will become successful in that field. But you can't cheat the time invested and expect the same results.[7]

When you don't know how to succeed, it's typically a sign that you haven't yet discovered the right mentors to show you the way. I genuinely believe that most people want to succeed. It's not because they don't have the will to succeed—it's because not enough people are adequately preparing for the success they desire. But in the end, you can't blame the lack of mentorship for your failure or success; it all rests on you. Always look at the person in the mirror.

Success is not an accident. Successful people don't just stroll around the neighborhood walking their dog and happen upon a bag of gold nuggets—that's a fantasy. Successful people, like the Rick Pitinos of the world, have spent countless hours gaining knowledge and acquiring skills that increase the value of their services.

Increased preparation equals increased value. It's not that complicated. If you had to undergo major surgery and could pay for the operation out of your bank account, who would you choose to perform the surgery, a world-renowned specialist or a first-year resident fresh out of medical school? Would you want a young doctor who would cost much less to save money but risk your life? Would you like to be lying on the operating table and hear the young doctor whisper to the anesthesiologist, "Pray for me; this is my first solo operation!"

Of course not. You would choose the specialist even if he charged 20 times more than the doctor who just graduated. Would the specialist be worth the extra money if your life was in his hands? You better believe it!

As leadership expert Burke Hedges says, "What you earn is directly proportional to what you learn."[8] You don't increase your value by winging or wishing for it. Successful people understand the importance of preparation. Remember, it's too late to prepare when the door of opportunity opens! It may take 20 years to become an overnight success, but don't stop learning, growing, and preparing.

It's time to stop making excuses. The ability and will to turn your dreams into reality are already inside you. The question is, are you willing to do whatever it takes to pursue them? Are you determined enough to do so?

FOUR WARNING SIGNS OF IMPENDING FAILURE

Here are four barriers and how to overcome them:

1. UNINSPIRING GOALS

Here's the challenge:

When most people set goals, they envision a particular amount of money, an object (like a new house), buying a piece of land, building a lake home, etc. All these and more can motivate you and others, but do they inspire you? There's nothing wrong with wanting better for you and your family. But if that's all that inspires you, I'm convinced your mind will change as you want these things to inspire others. Because, for the most part, material goals don't appeal to the core of what motivates the heart. Like New Year's resolutions, these unrealistic goals will end up on the shelf of boredom, never to be completed.

The solution:

Rather than envisioning an object as your goal, imagine how you will feel when you achieve the goal with all the strength in your imagination. That way, you'll be inspired to do whatever it takes to achieve that goal. Think of the lives you will touch and the value you will add to many people. Think of the difference you will make in inspiring others to achieve their goals. People, not things, are the actual value of life. Those successful people I know have realized it's not about what they can get but what they can give. I love the stories about blessing Mom and Dad with a new truck or car and providing fantastic trips they could have never taken without your generosity. Now, that turns on the passion. I have prayed for years that God will overwhelmingly bless us financially because my dream is to give millions away to bless others.

2. FEAR OF FAILURE

Here's the challenge:

If you're scared of failing, you'll hold back from taking the risks needed to reach your goal. For instance, you might skip making that crucial phone call because you're worried about getting turned down. Many dreams have died on the vine because of the fear of failure. Some are frozen in fear of making the wrong decision, which would lead to failure. If you don't decide, you will be wrong 100 percent of the time. Go ahead and decide—at least you have a 50-50 chance of being right.

The solution:

Make up your mind right now to decide that your possibility of failure is strictly temporary. Don't worry; your will and emotions will follow your mind's actions. Once you choose to "go for it," view any setbacks as temporary delays in your eventual success. Go ahead and accept the fact that sometimes failure is going to happen. Know this: your life is not defined by temporary circumstances that you (and others) might consider a failure.

3. FEAR OF SUCCESS

Here's the challenge:

Over the years, I have collected many books on leadership and success. Rarely do I find anyone discussing the fear of success. Suppose you become tremendously successful, and with that success comes enormous wealth. Would that be what makes you happy? Would your extended family pressure you to pay their bills for them? What if the success made you unhappy? What if you go bankrupt and all your friends turn away from you? Thoughts like this are common and can affect even the most highly motivated to sabotage their success. Some are honest enough to realize they couldn't handle a great deal of success with how they are presently. So, they can fear premature success, knowing how many have failed because they weren't ready.

The solution:

There was a man in the Bible who made a comment that speaks volumes to the subject. His name is Paul, and he said, *"...I have learned in whatever state I am, to be content"* (Philippians 4:11 NKJV). Rather than focusing on possible problems, consider how marvelous it would be not to worry about budgeting your living but budgeting you're giving. Instead of living with the fear of success, live with the excitement of helping others reach their dreams! Believe that God will not allow you to succeed beyond your ability to handle that success. Because you want His best, He will oblige you.

4. AN IMPRACTICABLE TIMETABLE

Here's the challenge:

Many people overestimate how much they can accomplish in a week, but underestimate how much they can achieve in a year. Because of this, most people try to do too many things in the short-term and become frustrated. Conversely, they view planning something over 12 months as long-term, which makes the goal seem too far away, allowing discouragement to set in.

The solution:

If you have a goal, consider using the 80-20 rule. Focus on 20 percent of tasks that achieve 80 percent of your desired outcomes. While bold, long-term timelines are essential, give yourself some flexibility when short-term planning. Remember that most goals require a realistic 2- to 5-year plan for true success.

Shortcuts always lead to cutting your future short.

HOW TO BOUNCE BACK UP

Have you heard the expression, "If you want to be the best, you must beat the best?" That slogan has been popular in the sports world for several years. However, no golfer, football player, baseball player, or other athlete in any major sport worldwide has uttered those words.

Another thought is that if you want to be successful, you should do all you can to learn how others have succeeded. Read their books, listen to their CDs, and attend their seminars—whatever it takes! Get to know your mentor and get in your mentor's back pocket. Don't be afraid to ask questions.

Yes, there is a resurrection side of failure. How do I know? I've been there. But that's another story.

Remember, it's not about how loud you shout, how high you jump, or even if you've been turned upside down. It's about how straight you fly when turned right side up each day.

7

CHANGE YOUR OUTCOME BY CHANGING YOUR ATMOSPHERE

Whatever a man wants badly and persistently enough will determine the man's character.

—*A. W. Tozer*[1]

Job lived a righteous and faithful life, but trouble still found him. Even though God blessed him, hardship came his way. The story of Job shows that, despite appearances, he lived in constant fear that his worst nightmare would come true. On the surface, it seemed like everything was fine, but deep down, Job was filled with anxiety, and that fear created an atmosphere that invited disaster. He focused so much on the worst-case scenario that it eventually happened. Job is a clear example of how negativity can shape our surroundings. Like a magnet, his fear attracted calamity into his life.

Yes, it is true that at the end of the story, God gave him "double for his trouble," but the fact remains that there are lessons to be learned about the importance of a proper environment.

LESSON 1. WE WERE CREATED TO FUNCTION IN A PROPER ENVIRONMENT

Merriam-Webster's dictionary defines *environment* as "circumstances, objects, and conditions by which one is surrounded."

I am convinced that God's greatest desire and our profound need is to share an enduring, Spirit-to-spirit relationship with our Creator. God knew how He would make His creation from the moment of creation. He also knew that man needed to be placed in an ideal environment. A proper atmosphere (environment) was crucial for him to function to his maximum potential. God prescribed an environment for everything He created before He created it. An ideal environment is one that God can fill with His presence.

God placed man in a perfect environment called Eden. Bible scholars universally agree that the root meaning of the Hebrew word for *Eden* is unclear. Strong's Concordance gives a translated definition: "as the garden of delight." Other Scriptures, such as Ezekiel 28:13 (NIV), describe it as "the garden of God."

In this prepared "garden of delight," three characteristics are essential:

- It was delightful and pleasant.
- It was a place where His presence touched the earth.
- God planted the garden, not Adam. God implanted and imprinted His presence in the perfect environment for man.

There were no church services, choirs, or worship services in the garden to "work up" God's presence. When God fills an environment with His presence, there is no need to spend an hour going through spiritual gymnastics for God to show up.

When something is placed in an environment that is not ideal, inevitably, malfunctions will occur. If you spend $60,000 on a new car and drive it into a lake to see if it will float, you will destroy the ideal function of the vehicle. A car was not made to drive into a lake. It was made for the open road. The same is true for humankind. Our life and fulfillment of purpose are only possible when we walk with God in the garden of delight (His presence).

There came a point in the garden of delight when Adam and Eve decided to step away from God's design. They chose to sin, and the consequences were separation from God's presence. Sin caused a break in the relationship, and man's opportunity to have unbroken fellowship with God was ended.

We must work hard to get into God's presence, but that was not what God designed for His creation. I do not believe that God ever intended that we would have to strive to enjoy His presence. It was not His intention that we needed to be in the right frame of mind or in a good mood on Sunday morning to enjoy Him. If you have ever thought some of the worship services you've attended have been boring, look at it from God's standpoint. A visiting preacher said once as he walked out of a Sunday morning service, "Lord, that was the most boring thing I've ever endured!" He said that the Lord replied, "Yes, you get to leave, but I have to stay here every week!"

God's original design was:

- Every morning we should wake up in His presence.
- We should be in His presence throughout the day, whether at work or at play.
- We should laugh and talk in His presence.
- We should go to sleep in His presence.
- Every aspect of our life is to be done in God's presence.

God had an answer to every human dilemma. In the Old Testament, He provided offerings and sacrifices for man to come into His presence and instructed Adam on the proper way to do so. From the Garden of Eden to the Temple of Solomon, God made provisions to deal with sin and allow man to know His presence.

When Jesus died on the Cross, He settled once and for all the issues for humankind. We can know the forgiveness of sin and a restoration of intimacy with God. We can now come *"boldly to the throne of grace"* (Hebrews 4:16 NKJV).

LESSON 2. THE DANGER OF THE WRONG ENVIRONMENT

I love to read simple stories that illustrate a great truth. My wife, Billie, can tell you I am constantly searching for interesting illustrations to share.

For example, the late evangelist and pastor Myles Munroe told the story of a small boy who wanted to play with his pet fish:

> So, he reached into the fish tank, caught the squirming fish, and placed it on the floor beside him. Then he returned to playing with the cars and trucks that were scattered on the floor around him. As he played, he talked to the fish about everything he was doing until he became so engrossed in his toys that he forgot about the fish. Many minutes later, he remembered the fish and turned toward his pet. The fish no longer moved when he touched it. Frightened, the boy ran to his mother with the fish in his hand.
>
> When his mother saw the fish, she quickly took it and put it in the fish tank. The boy watched carefully as his pet floated on top of the water. It was dead. When the mother asked her son what had happened to the fish, the boy innocently replied, "We were playing together on the floor when I noticed that he wasn't moving."
>
> Compassionately, the mother replied, "Honey, didn't you know that the fish can't live on the floor? God made fish to live in water."[2]

This simple story illustrates the importance of a correct environment. Just as birds need the resistance of air to fly and fish need water to live, man needs the environment that God designed for maximum functionality. When our environment is not suitable, we become like a fish out of water, simply flopping around and gasping for air.

There are several ways to judge whether you are in an environment suitable for maximum growth and productivity:

1. Do you have passion for what you're doing?
2. Are you constantly thinking about the past?
3. Are you excited or bored when you think about the future?
4. Do you know what fuels you for maximum growth?

If you are unsure how to examine and evaluate your proper environment, ask the following questions:

1. Can you remember when certain ideas and thoughts jump-started your creativity? How did that make you feel?
2. Do you have people who encourage or discourage you in your life?
3. When was the last time you had a dream that inspired you? What did you do with that dream?
4. Name the last book you read that inspired and motivated you to another level of productivity.

You can undoubtedly add to this list, but it is essential to remember that the definition of insanity is "to continue to do the same things over and over again, expecting a different result." Determine *not* to live the definition of insanity!

LESSON 3. CHANGE IS A CHOICE TO MAKE, NOT AN OPTION TO CONSIDER

Jim Rohn, leadership expert and motivational speaker, writes this about change:

> Any day we wish, we can discipline ourselves to change it all. Any day we wish, we can open the book that will open our minds to new knowledge. Any day we wish, we can start a new activity. Any day we wish; we can start the process of life change. We can do it immediately, or next week, or next month, or next year. We can also do nothing. We can pretend rather than perform. And if the idea of having to change ourselves makes us uncomfortable, we can remain as we are. We can choose rest over labor, entertainment over education, delusion over truth, and doubt over confidence. The choices are ours to make. But while we curse the effect, we continue to nourish the cause.
>
> As Shakespeare uniquely observed, "The fault is not in the stars, but in ourselves." We created our circumstances by our past choices. We have both the ability and the responsibility to make better choices beginning today. Those who are in search of the good life do not need more answers or more time to think things over to reach better conclusions. They need the truth. They need the whole truth. And they need nothing but the truth.
>
> We cannot allow our errors in judgment, repeated every day, to lead us down the wrong path. We must keep coming back to those basics that make the biggest difference in how our life works out. And then we must make the very choices that will bring life, happiness and joy into our daily lives.
>
> You can transform every area in your life—and it all begins with your very own power of choice.[3]

If you realize your environment is not conducive to growth, it's time to make changes. It's important to remember that before any major change of atmosphere (environment) can take place, you must be willing to change yourself first. When the seeds of knowledge are dropped into your heart, do they find a place where growth can occur to make necessary changes?

I'm sure you've heard the old story about two frogs being dropped into two pots of water sitting on the stove. The first frog was dropped into a pot of hot water, and he immediately reacted to the heat by jumping out of the pot.

The second frog was placed in a pot of cold water. The burner beneath the pot was turned down low, and the heat gradually increased. The water's temperature rose only a degree at a time. Change was occurring, but because it was gradual, the frog ignored it. He stayed in the pot until the temperature reached boiling! That frog was history!

The moral of the story is to change—or be changed. The first frog changed. He jumped out of the pot and hopped away to croak another day. The second frog was changed! He stayed in the water, ignoring, or perhaps denying, the gradual change in the water temperature until his goose, so to speak, was cooked.

This illustrative story vividly depicts two fundamental types of changes:

First, there are external changes. External changes refer to global shifts, such as the economy, stock market fluctuations, or technological advancements.

Second, there are internal changes. These are the changes over which we have control, including modifications in our attitudes, diet, exercise routines, education, and more. Both frogs in our story had control over staying in the water or jumping out of the pot. The first frog jumped out of the hot water, which saved his life. The second frog chose to ignore the warning signs and paid a heavy price for his choice—it cost him his life!

When you consider the history of the world, change has generally occurred very slowly. The Stone Age lasted thousands of years, and the Middle Ages lasted 1,000 years, well into the 15th century. But as the 20th century neared, change accelerated at a faster pace. From the

1850s to the 1970s, the Industrial Age hit, and change accelerated in America.

- In 1910, automobiles started rolling off the assembly lines.
- In the 1920s, radios were the rage.
- In the 1930s, the sale of telephones exploded.
- In the 1950s, televisions took over our living rooms.
- In the 1960s, we were introduced to the first industrial robot.
- In the early 1970s, personal computers moved from the mainframe to Main Street.

I have noticed that when God creates an atmosphere change in my life, He usually sends someone who will serve as a change agent. There have been times when I would shoot the messenger rather than hear the message!

Facilitators of change often agitate the people. You will need great courage if God calls you to bring about change.

When John the Baptist came on the scene, the curtain of prophetic utterance was raised after 400 years of silence; an explosion of change of unparalleled proportion was about to erupt in human history. Bursting on the historical stage was a scruffy-looking prophet named John the Baptist. He didn't wear a three-piece suit; instead, he wore animal skins, and his diet was grasshoppers and wild honey!

His message was "change and repent!" He was calling on the people to welcome the Kingdom of God. He declared that the past was over and something new would be born. By the hundreds, people flocked to the wilderness to hear this strange-looking preacher. He preached repentance from sin with evidence of fruit, even to the religious leaders of the day. They were plunged underneath the water, picturing the death of the Cross and the birth of a new beginning! You would have never picked this strange-looking man to bring such earthshaking change.

What did he get for his effort to proclaim the Messiah, the Lamb of God, was on the scene? He was beheaded! He was willing to pay the price to proclaim the good news. Learn this lesson: if you will be used to affect change, you can expect attacks, persecution, and ridicule.

Change agents like John the Baptist are pioneers who lead the way. Like the men who laid the track for the Continental Railroad, change agents become track layers for a new season of change. As one person described them, "They are the front car of life's roller coaster, human windshields in the front seat catching bugs in their teeth!"

History records the echoes of those who were willing to change and be change agents for God's glory:

- Noah constructed a boat in a place without water and in a world that had never known rain. Change was coming, and God warned the people through the words of this boat builder.
- Moses decided to leave Pharaoh's palace to lead slaves out of bondage. It cost him his privilege, power, and position. As you read the biblical record, you will note that Moses lived and breathed the supernatural.
- Amos the prophet was willing to give up his land, herds, and even his life to announce that change was coming to Israel.
- Isaiah survived the king's death and yet moved the nation toward God's greater will.
- Jeremiah saw the judgment of captivity coming upon his people. Even when he showed them the dark judgment to come, he declared the light of hope. For speaking the truth, he paid a heavy price.
- Peter was willing to give up his name, Simon (representing his past), and unleashed Pentecost on the earth.
- Saul (who later became Paul) was a Pharisee of the Pharisees, playing a significant role in his religion. God raised him up after being knocked off his donkey into the dust to turn the world upside down!

A look at more recent history shows us others who refused to be mired in mediocrity:

- Augustine, who saw the city of God.
- Martin Luther challenged the church to Reformation.
- John Wycliffe was a prolific translator of Scripture.
- Perpetua was one of the first women to die a martyr in the arena.
- Betsie ten Boom died at the hands of the Nazis.

Time and space would not permit me to list the thousands of men and women who testify to the price it takes to be a change agent.

Can one man change the environment, thus changing the way we live? Let me mention two who did: Nikola Tesla and George Washington Carver.

NIKOLA TESLA

> Nikola Tesla is finally beginning to attract real attention and encourage serious debate nearly 70 years after his death.
>
> Was he for real? A crackpot? Part of an early experiment in corporate-government control?
>
> We know that Tesla was undoubtedly persecuted by the energy power brokers of his day—namely Thomas Edison, whom we are taught to revere as a genius in school. He was also attacked by J.P. Morgan and other "captains of industry." Upon Tesla's death on January 7, 1943, the U.S. government moved into his lab and apartment, confiscating all his scientific research, and to this day, none of this research has been made public.
>
> Besides his persecution by corporate-government interests (which is practically a certification of authenticity), there

is at least one solid indication of Nikola Tesla's integrity—he tore up a billion-dollar contract with Westinghouse to prevent the company from paying him his huge royalty payments.

But let's look at what Nikola Tesla—a man who died broke and alone—has given to the world. For better or worse, with credit or without, he changed the face of the planet in ways that perhaps no man ever has.

1. Alternating current (AC). This is where it all began and what ultimately caused such a stir at the 1893 World's Expo in Chicago. A war was leveled ever after between the vision of Edison and the vision of Tesla for how electricity would be produced and distributed. The division can be summarized as one of cost and safety: The DC current that Edison (backed by General Electric) had been working on was costly over long distances and produced dangerous sparking from the required converter (called a commutator).

Regardless, Edison and his backers utilized the general "dangers" of electric current to instill fear in Tesla's alternative: Alternating Current. As proof, Edison sometimes electrocuted animals at demonstrations. Consequently, Edison gave the world the electric chair while simultaneously maligning Tesla's attempt to offer safety at a lower cost. Tesla responded by demonstrating that AC was perfectly safe by famously shooting current through his own body to produce light. This Edison-Tesla (GE-Westinghouse) feud in 1893 was the culmination of over a decade of shady business deals, stolen ideas, and patent suppression that Edison and his moneyed interests wielded over Tesla's inventions. Yet, despite it all, it is Tesla's system that provides power generation and distribution to North America in our modern era.[4]

GEORGE WASHINGTON CARVER

George Washington Carver was born during the height of racial discrimination in America.

> It is rare to find a man of the caliber of George Washington Carver. A man who would decline an invitation to work for a salary of more than $100,000 a year (almost a million today) to continue his research on behalf of his countrymen. He became a Christian early in his life and had an inventive mind. The southern farmers were suffering from overused land from the planting of cotton. Carver encouraged them to plant peanuts and sweet potatoes.
>
> However, the market was too weak for these crops, and Carver was severely persecuted for encouraging farmers to make such a drastic change in what they planted due to the lack of demand. Carver went into the fields early in the morning and cried out to God: "God, why did you make the peanut?" At age 63, he wrote: "Man, who needed a purpose, a mission, to keep them alive had one. He could be God's coworker. My purpose alone must be God's purpose. As I worked on projects that fulfilled a real human need, forces were working through me, which amazed me. I would often go to sleep with an apparently insoluble problem. When I woke, the answer was there."
>
> Over time God answered that prayer with more than 300 invented products that came from peanuts and 100 from sweet potatoes. Carver was credited for reviving the Southern economy. Presidents confided in him, and Henry Ford wanted him to work for him. He refused and continued to fulfill his calling as a change agent and a problem solver through invention.
>
> "My prayers seem to be more of an attitude than anything else. I indulge in very little lip service but ask the Great Creator

> silently, daily, and often many times per day, to permit me to speak to him through the three great Kingdoms of the world, which he has created, viz.—the Animal, Mineral, and Vegetable Kingdoms; their relations to each other, to us, our relations to them, and the Great God who made all of us. I ask him daily and often momently to give me wisdom, understanding, and bodily strength to do His will, hence I am asking and receiving all the time."[5]

The next time you flip on a light switch or open a jar of peanut butter, you can thank these two men, who were courageous in their convictions and not afraid to be used as change agents.

LESSON 4. A PROPER ENVIRONMENT EQUALS MAXIMUM PRODUCTIVITY

It's never too late to pause and examine your present environment. My goal is to serve as your "change agent," motivating you to realize that a proper atmosphere is crucial to maximizing your potential and thus increasing your productivity. Success is not something that happens suddenly. You plan for and define it as *"the achievement of something planned or attempted."*

To determine your proper environment, ask yourself:

- Is my current environment conducive to growth?
- Do I habitually challenge myself every day to learn something new?
- Am I willing to create a proper environment for maximum productivity despite any roadblocks others may put in my way?
- Am I willing to remove what is hindering my growth?
- Am I willing to start today?

Successful businessman and author Charles "Tremendous" Jones is well known for saying, "You will be the same person in five years as you are today except for the people you meet and the books you read."[6]

To release the treasure inside of you (potential), your environment must be constantly adjusted and evaluated. Your atmosphere is critical to your success! Why? Because your atmosphere is a large contributor to your actions. You will only succeed in an atmosphere that is conducive to success. So, you must create an environment or an atmosphere where you can flourish.

CHAPTER 8

WISDOM—DON'T LEAVE HOME WITHOUT IT

Not until we have become humble and teachable, standing in awe of God's holiness and sovereignty, acknowledging our own littleness, distrusting our own thoughts, and willing to have our minds turned upside down can divine wisdom become ours.

—*J.I. Packer*[1]

Imagine the following scenario: You've just settled into your new house. As you put some boxes away in the attic, you stumble upon an old metal box. You pick it up to see what's inside but quickly realize it's locked. As you stand there figuring out how to open it, you notice a key taped to the bottom. With a mix of curiosity and nerves, you unlock the box and find an envelope inside.

You open the envelope and read the note:

> I was worried that some of my greedy, unappreciative relatives would waste my money after I'm gone, so I hid a million dollars in the backyard. It's buried near the second large oak tree on the right—about three feet to the left and sixteen inches deep. If you find it, it's all yours.

What would you do if you found such a note? Would you continue storing boxes while thinking, *Someday, it might be nice to dig around in the backyard to see if I can find that box?* Or would you reason, *Since I don't know the person who wrote the note, I'm not sure it's authentic and trustworthy? I'll disregard the note.* Is that how you would respond? Of course not! You would stop everything you're doing, grab a shovel, and start digging as quickly as possible!

As useful as a million dollars might be, the Bible promises that God offers you something even more valuable—wisdom. Wisdom is more valuable than financial wealth because wisdom for living not only helps you increase your bank account but is also the key to relationships, job advancement, and spiritual success.

Proverbs 2:1-6 (NKJV) tells us:

> *My son, if you receive my words, and treasure my commands within you, so that you incline your ear to wisdom, and apply your heart to understanding; yes, if you cry out for discernment, and lift up your voice for understanding, if you seek her as silver, and search for her as for hidden treasures; then you will understand the fear of the Lord, and find the knowledge of God. For the Lord gives wisdom.*

You must search for wisdom as for silver, as for hidden treasures. In the book of Job, there is an interesting chapter where he discusses mining. You might think they weren't digging into the earth during Job's time. But they were! He says, where even the eagle's eye has never gone, going way down into the belly of the earth to mine out diamonds, gold, and silver.

Job asked the pertinent question, *"Where shall wisdom be found?"* Then, he begins to search for wisdom. He searches into the depths of the caves where gold is refined and discovers that wisdom is not there. He goes down into the ocean's depths, looking for wisdom, and does not find wisdom there. And then, in the last verse of Job 28, he writes, *"The fear of the Lord, that is wisdom…."*[2]

True wisdom is rarely found lying on the ground in plain view. Instead, it's a treasure that must be searched out, and those seeking it must often dig beneath the surface. It's not a difficult pursuit. It's fun to search for buried treasure, and it's wonderfully rewarding to find it.

WE MUST KEEP THE MAIN THING, THE MAIN THING

What is the main thing?

- It's not money.
- It's not fellowship.
- It's not a great marriage.
- It's not having a successful business.
- It's not having more friends.
- It's not going to church every Sunday.

No! The main thing is the principle thing—wisdom.

That immediately leads us to ask the question, what is wisdom?

> The New Testament word is *Sophia*, which means a concept to a Greek mind. To be wise meant to understand a concept, comprehend something, analyze something, think about it, and come to a comprehension of it. That's not the word in Hebrew.
>
> The word in Hebrew is *chakam,* and it means skill in living. The Hebrews are very concrete in their language and how they think; the Greeks are rather esoteric, mystical, somewhat transcendent in their thoughts, and a little spacey. So, you get these conceptual terms in Greek, but in Hebrew it has a

> very concrete meaning: skilled in living, to learn how to live skillfully, that is the issue. If you want to pursue something, pursue skillful living and pursue wisdom in every aspect of life.[3]

There are two important things to know:

- One is *knowing* what God wants.
- Two is *doing* what God wants.

It's not enough to mentally assent to the truth; putting that truth into action moves us to God's wisdom—not just "common sense" or "book smarts." God wants us to be wise men, not wise guys. He wants us to have wise words, not wisecracks. We have more educated people than ever before, but we do not have many people with wisdom.

It is one thing to have an education; it is another to have God's wisdom in your daily life. Some have said that we have become a race of clever fools. Some people are educated beyond their intelligence, and some are so smart that they lack any common sense. God wants us to have wisdom because we need it to understand life's daily problems and how to deal with them.

I once heard a very wise teacher say: "Godly wisdom is the ability to apply knowledge. You gain knowledge by looking around and wisdom by looking up."

Wisdom is the God-given ability to perceive the true nature of the matter and to implement the will of God in that matter. Godly wisdom will look at circumstances from God's perspective and apply His wisdom and will to whatever we face. Knowledge without wisdom leads to chaos. God's reality and human reality are often very different.

In Daniel, chapter 3, the three Hebrew teenagers were faced with a life-and-death decision. They applied godly wisdom. They were told that if they didn't bow to the statue of the king, they would be thrown into a fiery furnace (Daniel 3:15-18).

Natural wisdom says, "I'd better bow down. What good am I dead? I can't witness for the Lord; no one will blame me." Natural wisdom decides based on what is best for the individual and invokes the least amount of pain.

Godly wisdom says, "Take your stand. God commands you not to bow down to idols. Obey God and leave the results up to Him."

WHAT IS THE VALUE OF WISDOM?

WISDOM IS GREATER THAN MONETARY POWER. (PROVERBS 3:13-17; 2 CHRONICLES 1:7-12)

If you have financial difficulties, it's not because you don't have money. You don't have a money problem; you have a wisdom problem. You can have all the money in the world, but if you don't know *why* you have it, it will destroy you.

> *There is desirable treasure, and oil in the dwelling of the wise, but a foolish man squanders it* (Proverbs 21:20 NKJV).

The most popular television shows are the ones that promise the winners significant sums of money. Whether *Who Wants to Be a Millionaire* or *Minute to Win It,* these shows attract huge viewership. Why? The producers of the show claim that viewers are interested in more than just money, they also are stimulated by the intellectual challenge of the show. However, one veteran game show producer is skeptical. "Just try making the top prize one thousand instead of one million and see how long people remain interested. It's about the money."

People have always been fascinated with money, and for good reason. Money used properly can relieve stress, provide security, and help fulfill our dreams. Money offers independence and freedom of choice. Perhaps that's why Jesus warns in Matthew 6:24 (NIV), *"No one can serve two masters. Either you will hate the one and love the other, or you will be devoted to the one and despise the other. You cannot serve both God and money."*

Why did Jesus zero in on money, not sports, work, or marriage? Jesus understood the lure of money and knew what it would do to the human spirit if not controlled by the Holy Spirit.

Solomon, the wealthiest man who ever lived, certainly knew from firsthand experience the joy and benefits of great wealth. He also understood that money can easily be lost (Proverbs 23:4-5), can increase stress (Ecclesiastes 5:12), and can rob us of present joy in life (Ecclesiastes 5:13). Solomon gives us a reasonable financial goal in Proverbs 30:8-9 (AMPC) when he says, *"…give me neither poverty nor riches; feed me with the food that is needful for me, lest I be full and deny You and say, Who is the Lord? Or lest I be poor and steal, and so profane the name of my God."*

Solomon declares in essence, "God, I don't want so much money that I forget my need for You. But neither do I want so little that I am tempted to do something that would dishonor Your name. Give me enough money to meet my needs and to help others."

The average person believes the only way to gain financial independence is to earn more money, hope that a relative dies before all the bills come due, or appear on a game show and win big bucks.

Solomon provides insight and wisdom on the best way to achieve financial security. He observes, *"When good things increase, those who consume them increase…"* (Ecclesiastes 5:11 AMP). In today's language, he means, "The more you make, the more you spend." Godly wisdom says, "Whatever you earn, spend less!"

WISDOM IS GREATER THAN MILITARY POWER. (ECCLESIASTES 9:13-18)

> *I also saw under the sun this example of wisdom that greatly impressed me: There was once a small city with only a few people in it. And a powerful king came against it, surrounded it and built huge siege works against it. Now there lived in that city a man poor but wise, and he saved the city by his wisdom. But nobody remembered that poor man. So, I said, "Wisdom is better than strength." But the poor man's wisdom is despised, and his words are no longer heeded. The quiet words of the wise are more to be heeded than the shouts of a ruler of fools. Wisdom is better than weapons of war, but one sinner destroys much good* (Ecclesiastes 9:13-18 NIV).

US Army General Omar Bradley said about wisdom and military power:

> We have men of science, too few men of God. We have grasped the mystery of the atom and rejected the Sermon on the Mount. The world has achieved brilliance without conscience. Ours is a world of nuclear giants and ethical infants. We know more about war than we know about peace, more about killing than we know about living. If we continue developing our technology without wisdom or prudence, our servant may be our executioner.[4]

Power comes from wisdom, not from strength. This is such an essential principle that the writer makes it twice in this short passage. First, in verse 15, he writes: "*Wisdom is better than strength,*" and then in verse 18, we find these words: "*Wisdom is better than weapons of war.*"

This contradicts the idea that "might is right" and clearly refutes the concept of "the survival of the fittest," which is the basis for the theory of evolution. Although strength might indeed prevail in the short run, wisdom is much more profitable in the long run.

WISDOM IS GREATER THAN MENTAL POWER. (PROVERBS 4:4-9)

How do you get the wisdom kind of mental power?

Step One: A Right Relationship with Jesus.

People have said that if they could go to some mountaintop and sit at the feet of some wise man, then they would find wisdom. Many have tried that, and it didn't work. What person? We all need coaches and mentors. But the best Person is living inside you right now—Jesus Christ!

> *It is because of him that you are in Christ Jesus, who has become for us wisdom from God—that is, our righteousness, holiness and redemption* (1 Corinthians 1:30 NIV).

> *For this reason, since the day we heard about you, we have not stopped praying for you. We continually ask God to fill you with the knowledge of his will through all the wisdom and understanding that the Spirit gives* (Colossians 1:9 NIV).

Step Two: A Right Relationship with the Bible.

Have you ever just wanted to talk to the author of a book you were reading? How about a how-to book? You have the Author of the Bible living inside you!

> *How sweet are your words to my taste, sweeter than honey to my mouth! I gain understanding from your precepts; therefore, I hate*

every wrong path. Your word is a lamp to my feet, a light on my path (Psalm 119:103-105 NIV).

Let the word of Christ dwell in you richly in all wisdom, teaching and admonishing one another in psalms and hymns and spiritual songs, singing with grace in your hearts to the Lord (Colossians 3:16 NKJV).

GREAT REWARDS FOR READING GOD'S WORD

- The Word of God solves your mental problems. (Psalm 119:165)
- The Word of God cleanses your conscience. (John 15:3)
- The Word of God purifies. (Psalm 119:9)
- The Word of God corrects you. (2 Timothy 3:16)
- The Word of God solves every battle. (Psalm 119:98)
- The Word of God warns of pitfalls. (Psalm 119:11)
- The Word of God drives back the darkness from around you. (Psalm 119:130)
- The Word of God gives great joy. (John 15:11)
- The Word of God births the fear of God. (Proverbs 9:10)
- The Word of God creates a hatred of evil. (Proverbs 3:7)
- The Word of God is the Source of wisdom in your life. (Proverbs 2:6)

WHAT DOES WISDOM HAVE TO DO WITH ME?

God does not withhold wisdom from those who will pursue it. He wants us to have wisdom because it is important to us. His wisdom is not reserved for one group or class of people.

The following are three ways God's wisdom relates specifically to our life:

1. WISDOM IS THE VEHICLE TO GET US WHERE WE WANT TO GO.

Just as your car takes you to church, the mall, or to visit a relative, wisdom is the vehicle for getting you from where you are now to where you want to go. If I were to ask you right now, "What do you need more than anything else?" What would you say? Would it be more money, a stable home life, a spouse, new friends, or a better job? Above all else, wisdom is the principal vehicle for everything you want or need (see Proverbs 4:7-9).

Automaker Henry Ford asked electrical genius Charlie Steinmetz to build the generators for his factory. One day, the generators ground to a halt and the repairmen couldn't find the problem. So, Ford called Steinmetz, who tinkered with the machines for a few hours and then threw the switch. The generators whirred to life—but Ford got a bill for $10,000 from Steinmetz. Flabbergasted, the rather tightfisted car maker inquired why the bill was so high. Steinmetz's reply: For tinkering with the generators, $10. To know where to tinker, $9,990. Ford paid the bill.[5]

2. WISDOM IS ABSOLUTE AND THE OPPOSITE OF OUR NATURAL INCLINATION.

The Bible talks about two kinds of people: the wise and the foolish. Jesus talked about two men who built a house (see Matthew 7:24-27). One built his house on the rock, the other on the sand. They both had a choice of what kind of foundation to build on.

When the storm came, the man who had built his house on the rock discovered that the foundation was strong enough to withstand adversity. The man who built his house on sand discovered the strong storm overpowered his home, and it fell.

With that parable in mind, which would you choose? Everyone faces storms. Would you rather face adversity with godly wisdom or man's wisdom? Matthew 10:16 says, *"Be wise as serpents."* Wisdom is not an option; it's a requirement for godly living.

3. WISDOM EXTENDS TO EVERY AREA OF OUR LIFE.

The enemy wants to convince us that wisdom is just for a few and not everyone. He wants us to feel that God is not concerned about every area of our life. The Bible clarifies in the book of James that God gives wisdom to all who ask (James 1:5-8). He promises not to withhold wisdom from us, but we must go to Him and ask in faith, believing that we will receive it. God will never be upset or angry when we ask for wisdom, no matter how many times or situations we need it.

The words of Eleanor Roosevelt ring true: "One's philosophy is not best expressed in words. It is expressed in the choices one makes. In the long run, we shape our lives and ourselves. The process never ends until we die. And the choices we make are ultimately our responsibility."[6]

Isaiah knew it: In Isaiah 29:14 (NIV), the prophet says, "*...the wisdom of the wise will perish, the intelligence of the intelligent will vanish.*" In that chapter of Isaiah, the king was engaged in a grave matter. He had gathered all his wise men and counselors together and asked for their wisdom. But God, who was going in a different direction, says in essence, "I'll bring all their understanding to nothing. No matter what plans they make according to the wisest instructions they can find, I'll bring it all to a standstill."

Paul knew it: The apostle Paul shared the same sentiment in 1 Corinthians 1:19-20 (NIV), discussing the difference between man's wisdom and God's wisdom. *"For it is written: 'I will destroy the wisdom of the wise; the intelligence of the intelligent I will frustrate.' Where is the wise person? Where is the teacher of the law? Where is the philosopher of this age? Has not God made foolish the wisdom of the world*?" Paul is saying, "*What has all of the world's wisdom produced?*" In the same verse, his answer is: *"Has not God made foolish the wisdom of this world?"* Even when we combine all the wisdom of men and all their marvelous scientific achievements through thousands of years of recorded history, they can't save one soul or change one human life. God says that human wisdom is foolishness. Man's wisdom has failed to solve basic human problems and cannot provide inner peace. Modern psychiatry, apart from God, says that we can solve our problems. Someone has said, "Modern psychiatry just simply arranges our hang-ups so that we can be unhappy more efficiently."

James knew it: James also clarifies that godly wisdom differs from earthly wisdom (James 3:13-18). James is telling us that there are two sources of wisdom. One is godly, and the other is earthly or demonic. One is truthful, and the other is lies. One creates order and peace, while the other creates confusion. You can't live in an ungodly manner and expect to have peace in your life. It just does not work that way. The lack of godly wisdom causes all kinds of problems. The lack of godly wisdom causes chaos and confusion. Do you have confusion in your home? Do you have chaos at work? Is your life a mess? If there is no order and peace, then you lack godly wisdom. How does a person know if they have godly wisdom? When there is godly wisdom, there is truth, there is peace, there is order, there is mercy, and there is compassion. Knowing God's plan for your life is impossible without His wisdom. The world's wisdom cannot answer because it doesn't know where you came from, why you are here, and where you will go when you die. God says I will give you one problem to solve to show humanity's futility. Find Me! Man, without revelation or faith in God, starts looking.

The astronomer who doesn't know God could have all the wisdom this world could produce. He could spend a lifetime looking at the telescope, but he would conclude, "I didn't see God anywhere." Biologists who don't believe in God's wisdom will take apart pieces of plant life, study them for a lifetime, and still not find God in any of their samples. The philosopher will study life's eternal questions, but without God, they will conclude, "You were born, and then you die—the middle part is up to you."

WHAT ARE THE REWARDS OF GODLY WISDOM?

> *In whom are hidden all the treasures of wisdom and knowledge* (Colossians 2:3 NIV).

- Wisdom is the master key to all the treasures of life. (2 Chronicles 1:11-12)
- The fear of the Lord is the beginning of wisdom. (Proverbs 9:10)
- Right relationships increase your wisdom. (Proverbs 13:20)
- The wise welcome correction. (Proverbs 9:8-9, Proverbs 15:31-32)
- Wisdom creates currents of favor and recognition toward you. (Proverbs 4:8, Proverbs 8:34-35)
- Wisdom guarantees promotion. (Proverbs 8:15-16, Proverbs 4:7-9)
- When you increase your wisdom, you increase your wealth. (Proverbs 8:18,21)
- Wisdom makes your enemies helpless against you. (Proverbs 2:6-12)

In the book of Lamentations, we read, *"Through the Lord's mercies we are not consumed, because His compassions fail not. They are new every morning"* (3:22-23 NKJV). What a great way to start the day. You can't go back and live yesterday over again. What might happen tomorrow is out of your control, so don't waste your time worrying about the future. The only thing you can do is determine the choices you make today.

When you are determined to live a life based on godly wisdom, grounded in His Word, your life is tethered to solid rock, and you can't help but approach each new day with a positive outlook. When your outlook is positive, your choices become strong. If your outlook is negative, your choices become negative, and you will view life through the lens of negativity.

The following are *four keys* to making better choices:

1. Choose that today is going to be the best day of your life.
2. Make a choice that will propel you to another level of growth.
3. Choose to let go of the past.
4. Choose to take ownership and be a good steward of everything God has put in your hand.

Remember, your daily choices will either propel you closer to your destiny and purpose or move you farther away from God's design for your life. It's up to you how you want to live.

DAILY WISDOM DECLARATION

I encourage you to make a daily wisdom declaration:

> *Father, I realize my need for Your wisdom today. I confess to you that I am not as wise as I want to be. Please forgive me for not pursuing wisdom as I ought. I recognize You want me to have Your wisdom to guide me in every decision I make and in every relationship I establish. I pray You will fill me with Your awesome presence and remind me of the importance of daily wisdom. I desire to get into the flow of wisdom. I will consult Your wisdom before making decisions, not after. Set my course on the path toward Your*

wisdom, and in so doing, I will receive Your highest and best for me. I declare this in Jesus's name, amen.

Living according to God's wisdom doesn't just happen—it's a choice. We don't have to go it alone. God begins each day by granting us the freedom to choose how we will live our lives. Since God loves us so much and is relaxed enough to give us new choices each day, we can certainly follow suit and make the right choices.

9

THE NEHEMIAH EFFECT

Never give in, never give in, never, never, never, never—in nothing, great or small, large or petty—never give in except to convictions of honour and good sense.

—*Winston Churchill*[1]

Staying focused on your dreams during all the difficult seasons of life is a major key to defeating discouragement. Discouragement can affect anyone at any time, regardless of age or level of success in business or ministry.

I once heard it said, "When we board an airplane, the sky is overcast. But as the plane climbs up through the clouds, we emerge into a sun-drenched world far above the dismal and disappointing things of Earth. If we could only see our clouds from the other side, as we do when flying above them in an airplane, their radiant magnificence would take our breath and our worries away. These same clouds that are hanging low in your life and look so dark from the underside would look totally different if you could see them from God's vantage point."

Have you ever been so tired of the ministry that you wanted to throw up your hands and quit? Has the work been so overwhelming that you lost your joy and decided the best course of action was to try to muddle through the day? Many days, I get tired in the ministry, but I never get so exhausted that I want to quit. A discouraged person will be defeated, and a defeated person cannot help another discouraged person.

Consider Nehemiah's position after God told him to go to Jerusalem and rebuild the wall and was met with opposition:

> *...I prayed to the God of heaven, and I answered the king, "If it pleases the king and if your servant has found favor in his sight, let him send me to the city in Judah where my ancestors are buried so that I can rebuild it"* (Nehemiah 2:4-5 NIV).

> *Then I said to the nobles, the officials and the rest of the people, "The work is extensive and spread out, and we are widely separated from each other along the wall. Wherever you hear the sound of the trumpet, join us there. Our God will fight for us!" So we continued the work with half the men holding spears, from the first light of dawn till the stars came out. At that time I also said to the people, "Have every man and his helper stay inside Jerusalem at night, so they can serve us as guards by night and as workers by day." Neither I nor my brothers nor my men nor the guards with me took off our clothes; each had his weapon, even when he went for water* (Nehemiah 4:19-23 NIV).

Now you know how Nehemiah must have felt. He realized the enemy was trying to attack not only from without but also from within. God had given him a clear vision to head up a project that appeared harmless, innocent, and relatively simple. What could be so hard about building a wall around the city?

As many of us have, Nehemiah is learning that a plan does not always work out how we think it should. The more he tried to alleviate the problem, the greater it became. The enemies started with sarcasm, mockery, and finally, open opposition and criticism of the work. Before it was over, they eventually tried to kill him (see Nehemiah chapter 4).

Have you ever had the experience of trying to solve a problem and it got worse right before your eyes? The more you prayed, the more difficult it became? At times, we may not have any tangible evidence that things will ever improve. During those times, it is helpful for us to know that everyone must go through unavoidable seasons of life. It's always our choice whether to "go" through those seasons or "grow" through them.

In Nehemiah chapter 4, things get more complicated for this anointed building contractor. Remember, Nehemiah was not a prophet, priest, or king—he was the cupbearer to King Artaxerxes. He was an important officer in the royal court. He had the critical responsibility of administrator and leader of men. When he learned the deplorable state of the wall around Jerusalem and the broken-down condition of the gates, he sought permission from the king to return to the city to organize the work, repair the damage, and restore order.

After arriving in Jerusalem, under the cover of darkness, Nehemiah went around the wall, observing the damage and condition of each gate. His name means "Jehovah is consolation." After he toured the damage, he would need all the consolation he could get because the conditions were worse than he had imagined.

Regardless of the challenge before him, Nehemiah was:

- A man of vision.
- A man of action.
- A man of prayer.
- A man who took responsibility for his burden.
- A man of stability and integrity.
- A man of dedication and perseverance.

If it was a harmless project—why did it create such anger? I've taught over and over: "There's no such thing as a Divine operation without satanic opposition. And the greater the Divine operation, the greater the satanic opposition." But always remember, *"greater is he* [the Spirit of God] *that is in you than he that is in the world"* (1 John 4:4 KJV).

Considerable detail is given to the account of events concerning repairing the gates and rebuilding the walls. Nehemiah's passion and dedication were focused on this responsibility. These lessons from Nehemiah's life will serve you well and empower you to overcome insurmountable odds.

> *But when Sanballat, Tobiah, the Arabs, the Ammonites and the people of Ashdod heard that the repairs to Jerusalem's walls had gone ahead and that the gaps were being closed, they were very angry* (Nehemiah 4:7 NIV).

Know that:

- When God is working, the enemy will find a way to disrupt your efforts.
- The enemy will never oppose orthodoxy, nor will he oppose creeds of religion. The enemy only opposes what he is afraid of!
- Satan is terrified of the Holy Spirit's power and the leadership of a person with a dream or vision full of the Holy Spirit. If our work does not attract opposition, we must determine whether it is in the power of the Spirit or the works of the flesh.

Nehemiah faced a problem of discouragement. What a difficult spirit to face. I don't know anything that will stop God's work quicker than the spirit of discouragement.

According to the Merriam-Webster dictionary, the definition of *discouragement* is to "to deprive of courage or confidence: *Dishearten*: to hinder by disfavoring. To *dis* means to take away. *Dis-connect* implies a stealing away of courage, a loss of courage."

The lights go out when you unplug an electrical cord from the wall, but they come on when you "connect" to a power source. When we connect to the Holy Spirit, He gives us the power to overcome discouragement. When pressure is applied on the outside, the Holy Spirit applies equal pressure on the inside to keep us from "cracking up."

Discouragement is real and should NOT be ignored.

By reading the account in Nehemiah chapter 4, you will discover the root of his discouraging circumstances. And it came from an unexpected source—the tribe of Judah!

> *Meanwhile,* ***the people in Judah said****, "The strength of the laborers is giving out, and there is so much rubble that we cannot rebuild the wall"* (Nehemiah 4:10 NIV).

Here was the tribe of Judah. According to the Bible (Genesis 49:1-8), Judah would be the Messianic tribe. Because of their royal lineage, one would have thought they would have had more courage than the others. This tribe was highly respected because they were the chosen ones through whom the Lord Jesus would be born. If the tribe of Judah was discouraged, then the other tribes would be more inclined to give up the project as well.

The enemy loves to drive a wedge among the people of God. He will always move inside if he can't stop the work from the outside.

They kept saying, over and over, we are all going to die. *"Then the Jews who lived near them came and told us ten times over, 'Wherever you turn, they will attack us'"* (Nehemiah 4:12 NIV).

Nehemiah's workers kept hearing those threats day after day. They were living too close to the enemy. You cannot constantly hear a negative report without having some of it rub off on you. What you are taking in and hearing, you will eventually believe, and it will act like a magnet drawing the very thing to you. Garbage in is garbage out!

Some people will tell you that everyone comes to them with negative thoughts. They are known for being negative, so they are open to receiving negative thoughts. They love hearing something negative about someone or a situation—it gives them a sense of worth, value, and superiority. Here's my advice: Stop receiving negative thoughts and stop giving negative ones. How simple is that?

FOUR REASONS THE WORKERS WERE DISCOURAGED

1. THEIR STRENGTH WAS GONE.

Nehemiah 4:10 (NKJV) says, *"The strength of the laborers is failing."* The word *failing* means stumbling, tottering, or staggering.

The building project started excitedly; as verse 6 says, *"The people worked with all their heart."* But as Nehemiah soon discovered, keeping the joy was another thing altogether. Just at the halfway point, the newness began to wear off. Sometimes, we get halfway through the job and want to quit. It's not much fun anymore.

A loss of strength takes an emotional toll on our bodies and will lead to discouragement. This is especially true of those who have a great purpose or vision yet whose identity is not anchored in Jesus but anchored in the very work they do. Sometimes, God will take away all our security to show us where we are. Your identity in life must be in Christ, not your accomplishments; otherwise, you can be easily discouraged. Celebrate your achievements but realize the Source of your strength and identity is in God. Life is full of change, and so are our successes and failures, but God never changes. So, drop your anchor in God's unchanging grace, and you will not be tossed around on life's seas.

Notice that Nehemiah 4:6 (NIV) says that the wall was built to *half its height,* and in verse 10 the workers were at the point of *giving out,* which suggests staggering, tottering, and stumbling. When physically drained, it is easy to become discouraged at the slightest problem. It's also interesting to note when the workers became fatigued, the became discouraged.

It is easier to become discouraged when a project's novelty wears off. The work becomes monotonous and boring before you know it.

Verse 10 says, *"…we cannot rebuild the wall."* They were ready to throw in the towel. These are the same people described in verse 6 as those who worked with all their hearts.

If you're feeling worn out, watch out! There is nothing more dangerous than trying to "run on empty." Look around you; everything needs fuel to operate. The human body is no exception. Burning the candle at both ends sounds noble, but it will cost you. Without a doubt, tiredness can open you up to discouragement. More mistakes have been made when decisions were made at the "low point" of life. One of my mentors reminded me often that when we are physically tired, we are more open to becoming discouraged. Our minds will begin to imagine things that are not true, and little issues will become unsolvable. Our doubts and fears take on a whole new level of intimidation.

2. THEIR VISION WAS OBSCURED.

Nehemiah 4:10 says, *"There is so much rubble…."* They were saying that despite all the work, much more must be done. They could only see all the rubble, not the goal anymore. The more they looked at it, the bigger the job became.

Lack of strength leads to loss of vision. The adage goes, "Unless you change direction, you are likely to arrive at where you are headed."

Nehemiah's workers were learning a hard lesson. Before the wall could go up, the foundation had to be laid, and for that to happen, the rubbish had to be cleaned out. Many people want a strong Christian walk before cleaning out the rubbish of past hurt, bitterness, and unforgiveness.

When we become preoccupied with the problem, we become blind to the provision. Often, we are overwhelmed with the assignment because we are looking too far into the future. When we look at others' success, we become convinced we can never achieve this or that. Just remember that where you are now is where they were once. Clearing things down to the foundation is the only way to ensure the superstructure of your building will be secure.

3. THEIR CONFIDENCE WAS SHATTERED.

Some say the most devastating cause of discouragement is the loss of confidence. The walls were halfway up, rubble was everywhere, and they said, *"We ourselves are unable to rebuild the wall."*

When you lose your strength and vision, you will lose confidence. When you do that, discouragement is crouching like a lion ready to pounce.

Confidence may be shattered, and courage may be draining, but if God is for you, then YOU WILL NOT BE DENIED!

4. THEY FELT A LOSS OF SECURITY.

Nehemiah 4:11 (AMP) says, "*Our enemies said, "They will not know or see us until we are among them, kill them and put a stop to the work."*

The workers were unsure of the outcome. There are many areas of our lives that we hang on to for tangible security. One area is our jobs. Another is our friends and familiar circumstances. We are thrown into the pit of discouragement if we lose any of these.

Sometimes there is a feeling that no one else knows or understands. In fact, everyone faces discouragement from time to time. The great apostle Paul demonstrates how we should respond:

> *We are troubled on every side, yet not distressed; we are perplexed, but not in despair, persecuted but not forsaken, cast down, but not destroyed* (2 Corinthians 4:8-9 KJV).

No matter what's going on around you or what the fears are in you, always remember *"Nevertheless, God."* (See 2 Corinthians 7:6.)

What he is saying is very simple: "I may get knocked down, but I am not knocked out." I will keep moving toward the goal.

NEHEMIAH'S RESPONSE

How Nehemiah responded is the most critical part of his story.

It sure looked like the enemy was going to win in chapter 4. One thing you will notice is Nehemiah did not ignore discouragement. You can't ignore it. It's like ignoring a flat tire. Pray all you want, drive all you want; you will never get air back into it. You must stop and fix it. It's the same way with discouragement.

Nehemiah, like all good leaders, met discouragement head-on.

FIVE KEYS TO NEHEMIAH'S LEADERSHIP EFFECT

EFFECT 1 – NEHEMIAH POINTED THEM TOWARD A GOAL.

The builders had been scattered all over Jerusalem, yet they were still separated from their families. In Nehemiah 4:13 (NIV), he says, *"I stationed some of the people behind the lowest points of the wall at the exposed places, posting them by families, with their swords, spears and bows."* He gave them a common goal—self-preservation.

He turned their attention away from themselves, a sure sign of self-pity. He said to get together with your families and stay together as a family unit. (The home should be a fundamental source of encouragement.)

You will notice that Nehemiah stopped the work for a brief time. Sometimes, it's helpful to take a break. Step back from the work and spend a few days with the Lord. During this time, it's incredible how God can help us gain a clear vision of our goals and refresh us with His presence. Sometimes, you need to come aside before you come apart. Getting alone with your spouse and getting away from it all in times like these is the best way to reenergize for your future.

One of the sure ways discouragements attack us is through loss of focus. When we lose our focus, we lose the compass of our life. Focus keeps us moving in the right direction. If you are in the valley of discouragement, stop long enough to ask this question: *What do I want?*

I am amazed at how many people can't answer that question. If you don't know what you want to do with your life, it's impossible to help you.

Nehemiah knew:

- His purpose and mission: *"For the Son of Man came to seek and save those who are lost"* (Luke19:10 NLT).
- What he had to offer: *"The thief does not come except to steal, and to kill, and to destroy. I have come that they may have life, and that they may have it more abundantly"* (John 10:10 NKJV). Nehemiah had a sense of destiny.
- That successful achievers were detail oriented: *"For which of you, intending to build a tower, does not sit down first and count the cost, whether he has enough to finish it"* (Luke 14:28 NKJV).

EFFECT 2 – NEHEMIAH POINTED THEM TOWARD THE LORD. (SEE NEHEMIAH 4:14.)

The workers were looking at the rubble instead of looking at the Lord. He said to them: *"Remember the Lord..."* How do we remember the Lord? By what the Lord has said.

Every time the enemy attacks, stand fast and remind the enemy what God has told you. I want you to know it's okay to tell the enemy to "go to hell" back where he came from. Don't be bullied by the enemy. When he knocks on the front door of your life, ask Jesus to answer the door for you. You'll be amazed how quickly the enemy will disappear. Go back and rehearse the prophetic words you have been given. Pull out cards or notes that someone gave you as words of encouragement. Speak those promises out loud like you mean it; let your ears hear the words coming out of your mouth.

Call to mind who God is: *"great and awesome."*

When discouragement comes, remember that God oversees your life and is in total control. God is greater than any opposition you or they could face. People who are discouraged think of mainly one thing—themselves. Remember, when the rubble becomes so great that it blots out the face of God, it's time to stop what we are doing, punch a hole in the mountain of rubbish, and see God!

EFFECT 3 – HE POINTED THEM TOWARD A BALANCE—TO BUILD AND TO BATTLE. (SEE NEHEMIAH 4:15-17.)

A job must be done on the wall, but there must be a balance. Keep your tools handy, and keep your swords handy, too! Some only want to battle all the time. Others want to ignore the enemy altogether and hope he will go away.

Half of the people worked, and the other half kept watch. Those who worked used one hand to build the wall; conversely, they carried a weapon. They worked together as a team.

The enemy will always try to attack at the most vulnerable point. So, Nehemiah posted guards at the weakest spots. By doing so, he showed the enemy he would not be intimated, encouraging the people to stand firm and not be afraid.

The enemy wants us to stop the work on the wall (your purpose and destiny) and think about him. We must keep on with the work (our assignment) and, at the same time, be watchful and alert to what the enemy is up to.

Pastor David Wilkerson says:

> Very simply, that the spirit of discouragement is Satan's most potent weapon against God's elect. Most often, he uses it to try to convince us we've brought God's wrath upon ourselves by not measuring up to His holy standards. But the apostle Paul urges us not to fall prey to the devil's snare: Lest Satan should get an advantage of us, for we are not ignorant of his devices. (2 Corinthians 2:11). Paul is saying you have to see your discouragement for what it really is! It's a demonic weapon, an arrow that Satan shoots at you from his quiver to get you to doubt yourself. He knows he can't tempt you to turn away from Jesus. So he swamps you with vicious lies to make you think you'll never be good enough to serve Christ. He wants to get you so downcast that you'll want to throw in the towel.[2]

EFFECT 4 – NEHEMIAH POINTED THEM TOWARD A RALLYING POINT. (SEE NEHEMIAH 4:19-20.)

In the natural, the workers' rallying point was a particular place. It's also an essential spiritual principle for us to remember.

- *The place* in the natural was wherever the sound of the trumpet was coming from. It was important for everyone to know what the sound of the trumpet meant. The last thing you want to happen is for some to charge while others are retreating. *"If the bugler doesn't sound a clear call, how will the soldiers know they are being called to battle?"* (1 Corinthians 14:8 NLT).

- *The principle* is: Don't fight alone. It's still true today. We need others in the battle. We all need a rallying point, a close friend or a family member who can stand with us when the enemy attacks. One of the enemy's tricks is to tell you that no one else cares or understands what you are going through. When we feel this way, discouragement sets in. There is nothing worse than the feeling of aloneness. We all need someone who can come alongside and encourage us. Remember Elijah? In 1 Kings 19, God gave him a young man named Elisha to minister to him. God gave David Jonathan in his darkest hour.

I love the Scripture in Ecclesiastes 4:9-10 (NKJV), "*Two are better than one, because they have a good reward for their labor. For if they fall, the one will lift up his companion. But woe to him who is alone when he falls; for he has no one to help him up.*" We need each other. There are two things a true believer can never say: I do not need you, and you do not need me.

EFFECT 5 – NEHEMIAH ENCOURAGED THEM TO SERVE ONE ANOTHER. (SEE NEHEMIAH 4:21-24.)

In these verses, he was saying, in essence, to serve one another and to assist each other. There was so much pressure that they didn't even have time to change clothes. Ask God to point you to someone you can serve. Some of these folks worked, and some watched for the enemy, but they cared for something or someone besides themselves. In other words, they were all in it together. We all benefit when we have a "Three Musketeers" attitude. "One for all, and all for one." But remember, it begins with you (one for all) being a team player, protecting and serving the team.

Bible teacher Brian Bill said, "When you think about it, most of us are just halfway, if even that, in our Christian lives. We're aware of the rubble and the mess. And, like the wall workers, it's so easy to get discouraged and not remember the Lord, who is great and awesome."[3]

Jesus understands that we have a capacity not to forget and that many of us default to discouragement. Discouragement is an internal disease, but it is not incurable. It may be tough to handle, but it is not impossible.

If you are in the valley of discouragement, beware of the demonic trap set for you. You must always be on guard. There are several steps you can take right now to climb out of the valley:

- Go to prayer, giving the Holy Spirit time to do His work! Don't worry about what the enemy tries to dump into your mind; pray.
- The first thing the Spirit will do when He comes is expose all of satan's lies! Have faith that God's promises are greater than satan's lies.
- Find a friend and be honest about your emotional state. If they don't understand, find one who does.
- Make a list of all the blessings in your life and thank God for each of them out loud.
- Don't hide things from your mentor. A mentor can't help if not informed of what's happening in your life. Remember, two are better than one.
- Sometimes, God doesn't change your situation because He wants to change your heart. And when your heart changes, so will your situation.

Get back to work, but don't forget your sword!

And always remember what Nehemiah says in chapter 4, verse 20:

"Our God shall fight for us!"

10

PROBLEMS, PROBLEMS

ALL GOD'S CHILDREN HAVE THEM

Leaders think and talk about the solutions. Followers think and talk about the problems.

—*Brian Tracy*[1]

No one is exempt from problems. The problem most of us have is that we don't know what to do with them when they suddenly appear.

Consider the story of the farmer:

> An old farmer had plowed around a large rock in one of his fields for years. He had broken several plowshares and a cultivator on it. After breaking another plowshare one fall and remembering all the trouble the rock had caused him through the years, he finally determined to do something about it. When he put his crowbar under the rock, he was surprised to discover that it was only about six inches thick and that he could break it up easily.
>
> As he was carting it away, he had to smile, remembering all the trouble that the rock had caused him and how easy it would have been to get rid of it sooner. There is often a temptation to bypass small obstacles when we're in a hurry to get a large problem solved. We simply don't want to stop and take the time to deal with it now. Like the old farmer, we "plow" around it.

> Usually, we tell ourselves that we'll come back to it later. What often happens is that we never do. If the obstacle is of a type that will keep reappearing over and over, we're usually better off taking the time to fix it and be done with it. If we are tempted to go around it time and time again, we best stop and ask ourselves if the cost, in time, money, and trouble are worth it.[2]

CONSIDER FOUR CRITICAL STATEMENTS ABOUT PROBLEMS

1. ALL GOD'S CHILDREN HAVE PROBLEMS.

Learn problem-solving skills if you want to be a hero in your organization. You will be amazed how many people will search you out for help. Why? People don't like problems and will do everything possible to avoid them. They will place the reins of leadership in your hands if you are willing to take them. When you can either tackle their problems or are willing to spend the time necessary to train them to solve their problems, you become the local hero! Your willingness to help others solve problems will make you valuable to the organization. Even if the company downsizes, you would be the last to go! Think about what makes you valuable. I submit to you that you can face and resolve issues with wisdom.

People will always have problems, and they will always seek out others to help them! Where do most people often turn for help with a problem?

- Family Members: 56%
- Friends: 43%
- The Bible: 38%
- Other Books: 22%

- Minister or Priest: 16%
- Tapes by Leaders: 7%
- Boss or Employer: 6%
- Counselor: 4%

When we honestly look at where people seek help, we realize most of the time, family members, who are at the top of the list, can't help. As a pastor, I'm certainly not discouraging going to your family. Still, I have observed over many years of ministry that usually they can't resolve issues, only patch things up. Sometimes we look at people and wish we were them because they don't have the problems we do, right? Well, the truth is, we all have them, no exceptions. It doesn't matter how rich you are, how much education you have, how big your business may be, or how many awards you have won; problems are a *fact of life!*

Each generation has its own unique set of problems. We should remember well-known radio celebrity Paul Harvey's words: "In times like these, it is always helpful to remember that there have always been times like these."

2. SUCCESS IS ALWAYS BIRTHED OUT OF THE WOMB OF PROBLEMS.

The next time you see a bird flying, remember that the wind's resistance gives it the lift to fly higher. Without currents and withdrawn air, the bird would fall to the ground, unable to fly.

The same law—that resistance is necessary for success—applies to us. If our lives were free of all problems and obstacles, our opportunities and possibilities for more tremendous success would be eliminated!

Necessity Is the Mother of Invention

> It has been rightly said that necessity is the mother of inventions. Most of the inventions and discoveries owe their successful operation to necessity. Unless there is want, we cannot struggle

to attain the goal. The history of human progress in all walks of life is the history of man's endeavour to reach new goals.

When man felt hungry, he started hunting and tilled the land. The need for shelter leads the man to build huts and houses. The need for quick travel resulted in the invention of the fastest means of transport, making the world short. At the time of necessity, the human mind, which is creative and imaginative, thinks in a very quick manner.

In this age of science, where a race is going on, deadly weapons are being manufactured due to necessity. The fear of the enemy has forced the power-hungry countries to invent such destructive weapons of death. Too often, those weapons are in the hands of those who don't understand or care about the value of life.

As new needs arise, fresh methods are devised to meet them. New plans are hatched to find solutions to different problems. Necessity makes us bold, zealous and eager enough to fulfil our needs. Necessity is a blessing in disguise.

What is impossible in today's world? It seems there are no limits to what man can accomplish. Man can achieve anything he wants, provided he puts in hard labour and sincere efforts. Where there is a will there is a way. Constant efforts do bear fruit. Where there is any necessity, there is some invention, some research, to fulfill that necessity. All our inventions and discoveries are the direct result of our pressing needs.[3]

3. MAKE PROBLEMS YOUR FRIENDS, NOT YOUR ENEMIES.

God created you to be a problem solver. Please don't run from problems, embrace them as a doorway to a new level of opportunity and promotion. God gave you eyes to see, ears to hear, and a mind to think.

It's important to understand that your assignment on planet Earth is to find and solve a problem. Just as ministers solve spiritual problems, dentists solve dental problems, and lawyers solve legal issues, your assignment revolves around problem solving in your arena.

Jesus lived this principle. When confronted by the Pharisees concerning His assignment, He explained that He was called only to those who recognized their insufficiency and need of Him. When He met the "woman at the well" (see John chapter 4), He did not ask her to take Him into town to evangelize the city. His assignment was to introduce life-giving water to one woman and change her life. She had her problem solved. In turn, she became a living, breathing solution to the entire city; as the Bible records, a revival burst into flame because of her testimony.

Often when counseling a couple or individual, I ask a question. The question is intended to let them know just how important they are. I'll ask, "Don't you think I have more important things to do with my life than sit here and spend my morning with you?"

Almost every time, they'll look down, feeling guilty for taking my time, and answer, "Yes, I know you have more important things to do."

Then I make them look me in the eyes, and I reply, "No, I don't, because you are the most important person in my life right now; you're my assignment from God." This usually brings tears to their eyes because they finally realize how important they are to God.

All great leaders have had to overcome tremendous challenges (problems) in their lives. History is filled with examples of men and women who faced difficulties and challenges, yet despite it all, became great leaders. Whether it was physical handicaps, growing up in abject poverty, or educational limitations, they somehow found the resolve to overcome.

Likewise, the Bible is filled with everyday people who did uncommon things, men and women like you and me, who lived in a different generation with its own set of challenges. They did not run from the problem but toward the solution!

A few examples:

Noah became a leader determined to trust God despite opposition.

In Genesis 7:1 (NASB1995), God grieves over humanity's wickedness. While everyone around Noah had fallen into the darkness of sin, the Lord said of Noah, *"...for you alone, I have seen to be righteous before Me in this time."* Always remember, it's never right to do wrong or wrong to do right.

Abraham demonstrated that leaders are not afraid to embrace the unknown.

In Genesis 12:1 (NIV), God approaches Abraham and tells him, "*Go from your country, your people and from your father's household to the land I will show you.*" Abraham was unafraid to leave his comfort zone and travel to an unknown country. Successful leaders are likewise unafraid of uncertainty because they know that unless they are willing to trust God, they will never find the Land of Promise.

Joseph endured despite difficult circumstances.

The story of Joseph in Genesis 37 is powerful. Joseph faced many hardships, including being sold into slavery by his jealous brothers and his father believing he was dead. His master's wife falsely accused him and imprisoned him. While in prison, he interpreted a fellow prisoner's dream, but that man soon forgot him.

Despite these trials, Joseph rose to power as second-in-command in Egypt. During a famine, he saved his family from starvation. When reunited with his brothers, he said that although they meant harm, God used those events to position him to save lives. True leaders hold on to a vision that guides them through challenges, turning adversities into a path to purpose.

Moses was the kind of leader willing to speak truth to powerful men.

Yes, it's true. God must be compelling to get Moses to act in Exodus 3. At first, Moses gives excuses as to why he isn't the right guy for the job. When he finally does answer his calling, Moses approaches Pharaoh and boldly passes on the iconic message: *"Let my people go."* The Israelites, Moses' native people, had been enslaved by Egypt, and Moses was the one enlisted to lead them to freedom. When the time came, Moses was willing to step up and lead.

Joshua teaches us that leaders lead by example rather than law.

In Joshua 24, after leading his people into a new land, Joshua offers the Israelites the option to either A) serve the God who they had always served, the one who had brought them into the land, or B) serve the gods of the surrounding lands. *"But as for me and my household, we will serve the Lord,"* says Joshua (Joshua 24:15 NIV). The people answer in unison that they will pledge their allegiance to God.

David saw a big problem (Goliath) and was unafraid to face it.

Everybody knows this story of David, the giant killer. In 1 Samuel 17, the Israelites are being defeated by the Philistines and their 9-foot-tall giant, Goliath. Goliath taunts the Israelites and challenges them to send him one man, and if that man should defeat him, the Philistines would become their servants. When Goliath mocks him, David says, *"You come to me with a sword, a spear, and a javelin, but I come to you in the name of the Lord of hosts...whom you have taunted"* (1 Samuel 17:45 AMP). With that, he slings a stone at Goliath's forehead and knocks the giant to the ground, dead. This confrontation was the beginning of "rock and roll." David took that "rock" and "rolled" Goliath to the ground.

John the Baptist was not afraid to confront the religious phonies.

John the Baptist, in Matthew 3, is baptizing people and preaching about the coming of Jesus. When a pretentious, self-righteous group of religious officials comes for baptism, he calls them out for what they are: *"a brood of vipers."* Paul the apostle asked a religious crowd, *"What, shall I become your enemy because I've told you the truth?"* Remember, when you speak the truth, make sure it's in love. It may not sound loving, but it's love if the motive is right and not designed to hurt but help. Even a message of judgment carries the message of hope when people are willing to change.

Jesus taught us that leaders are servants first.

One of the most powerful examples of servanthood came from the life of Jesus when He washed His disciples' feet in John 13. When He is finished, He says to them, *"You call me Teacher and Lord, and you are right, for so I am. If I then, the Lord and Teacher, washed your feet, you also ought to wash one another's feet"* (John 13:13-14 NASB1995). Jesus, of course, isn't talking about feet. He's talking about servant leadership.

Peter is a portrait of a leader who recovered from failure.

Peter, Jesus's most well-known disciple, denies knowing Him three times while He is being crucified. Jesus had predicted that He would do this, but Peter insisted he would never deny Him—even to death. When the rooster crows (as Jesus said would happen), Peter realizes what he has done and weeps bitterly.

In Acts 2, Peter gives the first sermon after Jesus's ascension into Heaven to a crowd of thousands of people. He had previously denied he knew who Jesus was before these same people. Leaders don't become discouraged when they fail, and they don't allow self-pity to create an atmosphere of failure.

4. LEADERS LEARN TO RECOGNIZE A PROBLEM BEFORE IT BECOMES A CRISIS.

Great leaders are rarely caught off guard. They have honed their ability to detect a problem before it escalates into a crisis. At the core, a true leader strives to fix the issue before it grows to immense proportions, impacting not just a few individuals (where the problem initially lies) but the entire organization. Great leaders don't avoid dealing with minor issues because, if left unchecked, they may turn into significant challenges.

In counseling with leaders, I often tell them, "You can't live in crisis." This counsel came to me when my mother was dying several years ago. Do I run home to Maine whenever there is any change in her condition? Do I send Billie Kaye to check on her? I was frustrated and confused until a dear friend said, "Paul, you can't live in crisis. Make the decisions as required to make them and trust God for His timing." That was great counsel for me. Because of my busy schedule, I couldn't continually change my mind about where to be. I don't mean to sound insensitive about a passing loved one, but the point is no one can function living in crisis.

How Leaders Emerge During Challenging Times

> Great leaders don't reach the height of success without facing their share of minor challenges and major crises. In fact, most outstanding *leaders* would say that working through difficulties made them even better. A truly great leader will rise to the top in troubling times when difficult decisions are made, and decisive action must be taken.
>
> It takes someone with a clear vision and unstoppable fortitude to lead an organization through its worst times, whether it involves economic troubles, public relations nightmares, or relationship failures.[4]

Consider the Case of Southwest Airlines

> How can an airline survive a government order to ground its entire fleet and shut down for days? After 9/11, all U.S. airlines were faced with this same crisis. One that succeeded

> through the difficulty was Southwest Airlines, already known for its outstanding customer service. Southwest's passengers, flight attendants, pilots, and ground crews were stranded across the country after the terrorist attacks. But unlike their competition, Southwest's leadership did more than just sit and wait. They encouraged employees to leverage their trademark fun approach to business and to help stranded customers enjoy themselves at the movies or the local bowling alley. And when the ramifications of the shutdown forced other airlines to cut staff, Southwest's then-CEO, James Parker, announced just three days after 9/11 that the company would be keeping all its employees and issuing a profit-sharing payment.
>
> Leadership characteristics like crisis management, creative problem-solving, and a strong belief in the company's vision saw Southwest through this unimaginable situation. The CEO also protected his staff, which ultimately led to a stronger airline.[5]

There are no big problems or small problems, only big people and small people. We should spend most of our time not focusing on the problems but on building up people who can take on any problem that comes their way!

Jesus spent most of His time developing a small group of men who would, in turn, change the world. They were able to see up close and personal how Jesus dealt with every kind of issue:

- They observed how He dealt with a religious system that was in total opposition to the grace of God.
- When the multitudes were hungry and there was very little food, this small group of men participated in a distribution miracle.
- They watched as He raised the dead, healed the sick, and mended broken hearts.

- They learned that love and grace can overcome the wrath of the law as Jesus dealt with a woman caught in adultery.
- You and I face no problem that He has not already addressed. When Jesus counsels us on how to deal with worry, we need to pay attention.

SIX KEY APPROACHES TO BETTER PROBLEM SOLVING

Most leaders desire to become more effective in solving problems. The following are six key principles that will help you avoid common mistakes and keep you on track to resolving challenges more successfully.

1. I HAVE NO CLUE.

You might find this an interesting statement, but it's where you must start. We don't know everything; we only believe that we do. For example, there was a time when the "Flat Earth Society" was very popular. Everyone just knew for a fact the earth was flat. There was just one problem with what everybody "knew." It must've been a shocking turn of events after the first explorer returned and stated you don't fall off the edge of the earth. Things changed, and what everyone believed had to change with it.

If you think you already know the solution, you prevent your creative juices from producing the proper remedy for the problem. It's always good to remember the famous words of the "great philosopher" Sergeant Shultz from the old TV show *Hogan's Heroes:* "I know nothing!"

Always remember the words of James 1:5 (NIV), *"If any of you lacks wisdom, you should ask God, who gives generously to all without finding fault, and it will be given to you."*

2.PROBLEMS ARE NEW GROWTH OPPORTUNITIES.

One leader found the word *problem* so negative that he banned its use. Instead of problems, managers were told to talk about opportunities. His attitude was right. The word *problem* describes the need to choose between alternatives. If you are baffled, that is usually because you are unclear about what you want to accomplish or unwilling to accept the right alternative, even when analysis makes the best choice obvious. If you look at the history of any successful organization, you will find that most innovative changes were born as solutions to problems.

3.LEARN TO ZOOM.

The "Zoom Out Principle" is when you separate the problem from your thinking and ask "Why?" and "What if?" Don't take it personally. Deferred judgment works best when you stand back and analyze the situation. After standing back and taking a realistic approach with critical thinking, you are ready to "Zoom In" and ask "How?" and "How can we fix this?"

4. MIXED NUTS ARE BETTER.

Utilizing all members of your team requires a diverse group of mixed nuts. Some can quickly grasp the big picture without knowing how to resolve the issue. They are just happy to be involved. You might think their questions are silly, but often those ideas lead to solutions. You also need fixers. The experts will take all ideas, combine them, and create a practical path forward. The fixers will help you operate more efficiently. Don't underestimate the importance of a bowl of mixed nuts to solve problems!

5. ASK, "WHY?"

When attempting to resolve a problem, asking yourself all the relevant questions is critical. Asking the right questions at the right time is a significant element in the process. It's just as important to ask questions as to find a solution. When asking questions, listen without deciding or judging.

> The most serious mistakes are not being made as a result of wrong answers. The truly dangerous thing is asking the wrong questions.
>
> —Peter Drucker[6]

6. READ THE RULE BOOK.

Rules and policies are in place for a reason. They should not become walls but doorways to make life easier and solutions faster. At the same time, rules may be outdated, considering changing times and circumstances, and must be constantly evaluated. Ask "Why?" to uncover the basis of the rule; it may be time to change or remove any outdated rule. Policies and regulations were put in place to help, not hinder. Walk slowly before running to fix something that isn't broken!

If you are always the problem solver and never teach those around you how to think and decide for themselves, you will create a co-dependent group of followers, so the following are a few suggestions:

- Never allow others to believe you have the only answer to the problem.
- Be a coach, not a dictator.
- Help others put their solutions down on paper.
- Listen to their input without interpreting or interrupting
- Help them to see the best solution and let them take ownership of it.

FOLLOW HIS EXAMPLE

Jesus was the most outstanding leader ever—and He dealt with many problems, ranging from staff issues to facing His death. How did He handle them?

- He was calm in a storm. (Mark 4:40-41)
- He took decisive action. (Mark 5:24)
- He instilled courage. (Mark 5:35-36)
- He gathered the facts. (John 6:1-5)
- He asked questions. (John 6:5)
- He didn't panic. (John 6:6)
- He had solutions. (John 6:10-11)

Author, teacher, and pastor Robert R. McLaughlin states:

> Every problem in life has a solution stated in the Word of God. God reveals Himself and His policy through the written pages of the Bible, which we call the Word of God, the mind of Christ, and the voice of the Holy Spirit. God supernaturally directed the human writers of Scripture, without waiving their personal feelings, human intelligence, literary style, or any other human factor, to convey His complete and coherent message to mankind. This was done with perfect accuracy in the original languages of Scripture; these very words bear the authority of divine authorship. Therefore, there is no such thing as a problem in life that does not have a solution in the Word of God.
>
> For the unbeliever, solutions are always related to establishment principles, for only in establishment principles can the unbeliever utilize virtue and make it a part of his life. Therefore, solutions for the unbeliever are limited because he

has no eternal or temporal relationship with God. Ultimately, then, problem-solving is the monopoly of the believer in the Lord Jesus Christ. However, this does not mean that unbelievers cannot solve problems but that they do not have answers to all their problems.[7]

You will only be remembered in life for two things—the problems you solve or the ones you create.

—Mike Murdock[8]

11

THINK ABUNDANCE

BREAK THE CYCLE OF POVERTY

The world is full of abundance and opportunity, but far too many people come to the fountain of life with a sieve instead of a tank car…a teaspoon instead of a steam shovel. They expect little, and as a result, they get little.

—*Ben Sweetland*[1]

Are you living life to the fullest?

In his book, *First Things First*, Stephen Covey asks a series of questions to help us determine whether we are truly living well:

- Do you have sustained energy and physical capacity throughout the day—or are there things you would like to do that you can't do because you feel tired, ill, or out of shape?
- Are you in a position of financial security? Are you able to meet your own needs and have resources set aside for the future—or are you in debt, working long hours, and barely scraping by?
- Do you have rich, satisfying relationships with others? Are you able to work with others effectively to accomplish common purposes—or do you feel alienated and alone, unable to spend quality time with the people you love, or challenged in trying to work with

others because of misunderstanding, miscommunication, politicking, backbiting, or blaming and accusing?
- Are you constantly learning, growing, gaining new perspectives, acquiring new skills—or do you feel stagnant? Are you being held back from career advancement or other things you'd like to do because you don't have the education or skills?
- Do you have a clear sense of direction and purpose that inspires and energizes you—or do you feel vague about what's important to you and unclear about what you really want to do with your life?[2]

When you think about living life to the fullest, I mean living well, what images come to your mind?

- A portfolio of stocks and bonds that generate enough money to live off the interest for the rest of your life.
- You must have a GPS to find your way in a larger house with so many bathrooms.
- A luxury automobile for every member of your family.
- Hopping on a private jet to fly to New York City for lunch with a few of your closest friends.

You may think, "That's not me; I'm not that materialistic." You may be the kind of person who believes success is not measured by how much "stuff" you acquire or how many goals you achieve. It doesn't matter what your definitions are, I have good and bad news. The bad news is that you may not accomplish every goal or acquire everything you want. The good news is that you can have more than you do now by confronting and eliminating a poverty mindset that has invaded the church, the home, the marketplace, and even the nations. The simple truth is that God wants you to live well and abundantly. For too long we have been discouraged by those who misrepresent the word of God through their greed, pride, and excess.

If you are unsure about what God wants for you, don't just take my word for it; consider the following Bible verses:

> *Keep this Book of the Law always on your lips; meditate on it day and night, so that you may be careful to do everything written in it. Then you will be prosperous and successful* (Joshua 1:8 NIV).

> *Blessed is the one who does not walk in step with the wicked or stand in the way that sinners take or sit in the company of mockers, but whose delight is in the law of the Lord, and who meditates on his law day and night. That person is like a tree planted by streams of water, which yields its fruit in season and whose leaf does not wither—whatever they do prospers* (Psalm 1:1-3 NIV).

You may think that those verses come from the Old Testament and represent only God's promise to the nation of Israel. He promised to reward their obedience with abundance and prosperity to demonstrate His sovereignty over heathen nations. Therefore, we cannot expect those promises to apply to us today.

Were God's promises of success only limited to Old Testament characters? I do not think so. Consider what the apostle John prayed for his friend Gaius in the New Testament in 3 John 2 (NKJV): *"Beloved, I pray that you may prosper in all things and be in health, just as your soul prospers."*

No doubt John wanted his friend to succeed in his spiritual life *("as your soul prospers"),* but notice that John did not limit his desire for Gaius's success to spiritual development. In its context, John wanted his friend to prosper in every area of his life. He wanted Gaius to experience living in abundance and prosperity. I believe it is God's desire for you and me to live the same way. This covers every time John uses the word *prosper* to mean "to have a successful journey or to accomplish your goals."

This is the same term Paul used in Romans 1:10 (KJV) when he prayed for *"a prosperous journey by the will of God"* to visit and minister to the Christians in Rome. You are mistaken if you think a prosperous journey means having first-class accommodations and a warm welcome (see Acts 27). Although Paul faced hardships on his journey, it was still prosperous because he achieved his objectives.

WHAT IS THE LAW OF ABUNDANCE?

Galatians 6:7-10 (NIV) tells us:

> *Do not be deceived: God cannot be mocked. A man reaps what he sows. Whoever sows to please their flesh, from the flesh will reap destruction; whoever sows to please the Spirit, from the Spirit will reap eternal life. Let us not become weary in doing good, for at the proper time, we will reap a harvest if we do not give up. Therefore, as we have opportunity, let us do good to all people, especially to those who belong to the family of believers.*

Stated clearly, the law of abundance is the continual creation of resources produced for us to enjoy.

And 1 Timothy 6:17 (NIV) says: "*Command those who are rich in this present world not to be arrogant nor to put their hope in wealth, which is so uncertain, but to put their hope in God,* ***who richly provides us with everything for our enjoyment****.*"

Specific universal laws are in operation, whether we believe them or not. If we choose not to accept them, they still work. For example, you may say, "I don't believe in immutable universal laws." But the reality is:

- The law of gravity works whether you believe it or not. You can choose not to accept it. But don't jump off a tall building or toss a bowling ball up to see if it will land on your head!

- The law of seedtime and harvest is a universal law. Once again, you don't have to believe it, but I'm glad every farmer in the world does. Without the law of sowing and reaping, we would all starve to death.
- The law of cause and effect is another universal law. Every action produces a result in exact proportion to the action initiated. A body at rest tends to stay at rest, and a body in motion tends to stay in motion.

Whether it's a universal law or a man-made law, breaking one can cause serious side effects. In your city, there are man-made laws that say you cannot "drive through a red traffic light." You may choose not to believe it or disagree with it, but my advice is always stop at a red light, or you will pay a heavy price.

Some view the word *abundance* only as referring to money. This is a great deception. Moncy is only part of the equation, not the whole. In my life, I have seen many people who have a great deal of money, but I would not consider them living in abundance.

My definition of *abundance* may be different from yours. I believe wealth and abundance are "provided for through an unlimited supply." Philippians 4:19 (NKJV) says, *"And my God shall supply all of your need according to His riches in glory by Christ Jesus."*

Abundance must be viewed considering the present need. For example, money may not be the present need. The need may be restoring a broken relationship, healing for a sick child, or a better job. Financial wealth is not the end in itself. God's ultimate will for us is that we are made whole.

The greatest needs people have cannot be solved with money. For instance, you can buy a health insurance policy, but you can't buy health. You can gain friendships with money, but can't buy true friends. You might even buy a preacher, but you can't buy salvation. And true love, well, that's not for sale either. If money can fix it, it's not a big deal because there are many things in life that money can't fix. Please don't misunderstand; I'm certainly not against having money and plenty of it. I'm only against having money controlling our lives.

In short, when we think about God's provision, we are not necessarily talking about people whom others would consider to be very rich in the things of this world. Rather, God's provision to me means succeeding in what each and every person is called and equipped to do in fulfilling their God-given purpose. That's true wealth.

POVERTY THINKING IS DIAMETRICALLY OPPOSED TO ABUNDANCE THINKING

What is poverty thinking? Poverty thinking is the opposite of abundance thinking. Focusing on what you do not have instead of being grateful for what you do have feeds the poverty mentality. The poverty attitude shows no gratitude and focuses all its energies on being resentful for what others have achieved. A poverty thinker plays the "blame game."

What they don't understand is that by thinking of "lack" and "scarcity," they are creating the very circumstances that cause a further erosion of any hope of abundance, which is a tragedy. There comes a point when you talk to a person with a poverty mindset in which they refuse to accept any concept of abundance. They do not recognize the importance of a positive attitude.

WHAT ARE SOME CHARACTERISTICS OF POVERTY THINKING?

I've identified four characteristics of poverty thinking: hoarding, living by the "pie principle," rejecting God's road map to abundance, following the wrong crowd. Let's examine each.

1. HOARDING.

Hoarding is taking things we don't need or too much of what we do need to balance our lives. The problem with hoarding is that it stops the cycle of giving and receiving. Affluent thinkers are happy with what they have and give freely to others because they know there is a limitless supply if they need or want more.

God does not give to us to fulfill our selfish motives, so we can hoard everything for ourselves. God wants to provide abundance. God gives lavishly to those who give lavishly. It's a spiritual principle. Luke 6:38 (NLT) says, *"Give, and you will receive. Your gift will return to you in full—pressed down, shaken together to make room for more, running over, and poured into your lap. The amount you give will determine the amount you get back."*

When he says, *"in full—pressed down, shaken together to make room for more, running over,"* all this is about how God wants to give back to us. When we give away what's in our hands, God will give what's in *His* hands! Believe me, His hands are bigger than ours.

And 2 Corinthians 9:8 (NKJV) says, *"And God is able to make all grace abound toward you, that you, having all sufficiency and all things, may have an* ***abundance*** *for every good work."* Notice the word *abundance.* God can make it happen for us. When? Always. Where? In *all things.* In essence, it is God's will that we never lack at any point and that there will be no deficiency, only sufficiency for all good things. We may go through a valley of lack for a brief season, but we don't stop there. How else will we know that God is our source and supply if we never go through the valley of lack? When a need manifests itself in our lives, God signals that the supply is already on the way.

God knew that the children of Israel would need food as they journeyed through the wilderness to the Promised Land. They grumbled and complained constantly about lack. They didn't realize that God's manna was already in place and ready to be released. *God has always had the supply before we realized we had a need.* God created air before He created Adam. When Adam took his first breath, the air was waiting for him. God didn't ask him to hold his breath for three days, nor does He ask that of us. His supply awaits us to acknowledge our need and cry out to Him.

The Bible clarifies that God does not pour out abundance because we deserve it or demand it. The blessing of abundance is based on our becoming givers rather than takers and doing things God's way, not our way.

2. LIVING BY THE "PIE PRINCIPLE."

The pie principle has been propounded by every source imaginable for decades. From Wall Street to Main Street, we have been told that planet Earth has limited resources. The media joined the chorus of negativity by informing us that we are running out of everything from oil, natural gas, trees, money, and other natural resources. Every time you watch the news on television, you are bombarded with negativity about scarcity and lack.

The pie principle stated: There is one pie with so many slices. Once you take your slice, that's all you'll ever get; don't ask for anything more. There's nothing left, and there is no such thing as abundance. Once the slices of the pie are gone—it's over!

If your perception of the pie principle is accurate, your world is fading fast because perception becomes a reality. Whether we want to believe it or not, what we perceive, we believe. Therefore, it is what we will receive. If you don't think God can bring something out of nothing, look around. Everything you see is a result of God's speaking from the beginning. Genesis 1:1 says, *"In the beginning God created...."*

Scientists tell us that the universe continues to expand at the speed of light. I believe it's because in Genesis 1:3, God says, *"'Let there be light'; and there was light."* And God hasn't turned the switch off yet. You may say, "Bro Paul, I don't believe that." First, it's my book. Second, maybe that's your problem, you don't believe it.

Almost all of us, at some point in our lives, get caught on the same treadmill of consumption that wearies our American souls. As soon as our "cup runneth over," what do most of us do? Why, we go out and buy a bigger cup! That means we are always living with the illusion of scarcity, constantly bemoaning the gap between what's in our cup and the rim. When we, of all the people on the planet, are the most blessed financially.

We serve the God often referred to as the One who meets all our needs. That is true, and He is more than enough. I'm sure you have heard people say, "Our God supplies all of our needs but not our greed." Many things have been said about God, some true and some not so true. We need to know what the Bible says about how He views abundant living. Our God is not stingy or cheap, only giving us just enough to sustain us. He is the God of abundance.

Consider the following: Ephesians 3:20 (NKJV) says, *"Now to Him who is able to do exceedingly abundantly above all that we ask or think, according to the power that works in us."* Every single word in that verse tells me one thing: God is more than enough!

> A story is told of a missionary friend who was trying to reach a group of people in Mexico. They faced challenges because the villagers had what he described as a scarcity mentality. The missionaries noted that these beliefs influenced their entire lives. For instance, parents would typically have only one child because they believed that having two children would divide their love in half, with 50% going to one child and 50% to the other. Heaven forbid if they had four children, as each would only receive 25% of their parents' love. This scarcity perspective suggests that there is only a certain amount of pie, meaning that the more people there are, the smaller each

> person's share of the pie will be. As a result of this belief system, the missionary found it very difficult to reach this group with the gospel because this scarcity view fostered a mentality of greed among the people. They felt that since there was only so much pie, they needed to ensure they got their share, or they would be left out.
>
> The missionary attempted to teach these people about God's way, which he referred to as the abundance mentality. For example, God does not have a limited supply of love; His love is abundant, flowing freely to all His children. God's love depends not on how many children He has but on how many children have Him. He has enough love and more for everyone.[3]

The moral of the story is to refuse to live with a scarcity mindset!

3. REJECTING GOD'S ROAD MAP TO ABUNDANCE.

God's instruction manual (the Bible) is not just a history book or a book of genealogies. It's our road to royalty and our destiny, purpose, and abundant-living destination. As you open the instruction manual, you learn the keys to success in every area of living, including family, church matters, dealing with difficult people, our health, both mental, emotional, and physical, all relationships, and, of course, money management. Those with a poverty mentality refuse to apply the instructions to break the cycle of poverty.

> *Whoever disregards discipline comes to poverty and shame, but whoever heeds correction is honored* (Proverbs 13:18 NIV).

Instruction or knowledge can only benefit us if we are willing to act. If believers act in faith in the Word of God, they can stand against the thieves of abundance, but only if we are willing to act upon it. I have met many so-called wise men who are poor and wretched. In their mind, they genuinely believe they are legendary. Yet, they have very little or no fruit in their lives to back up their so-called wisdom.

Many people make the mistake of judging themselves by their intentions and others by their actions. In doing so, they forget that the road to poverty and failure is paved with good intentions. One must realize that a good intention is the voice of the Holy Spirit communicating to our spirit the will of God in a particular situation. Then, our spirit communicates with our intellect, and our intellect agrees that the instruction it has received from the spirit is the right way to illuminate God's character in a world seeking workable truth. But, as a Christian, without an act of the will to believe and obey, we're doomed to fail.

James declares in chapter 1:22 that when we fail to follow through with corresponding actions to God's instructions, we deceive ourselves. We do not, however, deceive those who are trying to convince us the way of God is a better way of life than anything the world can offer.

4. FOLLOWING THE WRONG CROWD.

> *A hard worker has plenty of food, but a person who chases fantasies ends up in poverty.* (Proverbs 28:19 NLT).

An old leadership proverb says, "If you're going to carry someone's briefcase, make sure it's someone who is going somewhere." Attaching yourself to the wrong person will put you in the same ditch. When you associate yourself with people with a poverty mentality, who are always critical and negative, guess what you will become? A person who is always negative, critical, and doubting. A lousy attitude is like a virus that spreads quickly. All it takes is to be around people with a negative view, and before long, you wake up and wonder what happened to your positive attitude.

If you want to fly like an eagle, don't hang around with turkeys! A wise person once said, "Your friends will stretch your vision or choke your dreams."

Living with a poverty mentality is not equal to living in the worst part of town or just being broke. You may be challenged with a lack of money and resources now, but that does not mean you have to live with a poverty mentality. Being broke is temporary, but a poverty mentality is a thinking pattern that kills motivation, destroys dreams, stifles desire, and quenches your passion. You can rise above your current circumstances with a positive attitude toward abundance.

Take charge of your attitude—think abundance:

- Assess your current attitude and determine whether it's based on abundance or poverty.
- Be prepared to make changes to let go of negative thinking.
- Identify your most significant barrier to abundance thinking and analyze why you have never embraced the principle.
- Start today by counting your blessings to develop an attitude of gratitude for the things you do have.
- Stop focusing on what you don't have; focus on creating the circumstances that will attract abundance to fill your empty spaces.
- Stop "entitlement" thinking. The world does not owe you a living.
- Take control by taking responsibility for your own well-being. It is not up to someone else to make you happy.
- You are not a victim, so stop thinking like one.
- Don't be too hard on yourself. Everyone makes mistakes. Learn from it and move on.
- Admit it, forget it, and get back in it.

PERSONAL WORD OF TESTIMONY

I want to share a personal word of testimony to the truth of this chapter. I pray you will know there is no judgment or condemnation to anyone intended, only our thankfulness to God for His abundance.

Since we came to faith in Christ, Billie Kaye and I have desired to be givers. We have prayed for abundance in every area of life because of God's promise in John 10:10 (KJV), *"The thief cometh not, but for to steal, and kill, and to destroy: I* [Jesus] *am come that they might have life and that they might have it more abundantly."* We have worked very hard to make the right choices in our marriage, with our children, friends, health, and resources. Even though we have gone through periods of drought and failure, we determined by God's grace not to live there. We found the abundant strength needed in Christ to get up one more time. I could use hundreds of examples of God's provision of abundance in every area, but there's one that will serve well here.

Years ago, we bought and began to build Restoration Ranch. We committed to build as God supplied the funds so we would be debt-free when done. We had been practicing generous giving for years and believed God would supply it somehow. We sold a home we owned personally and gave the money to the ministry so we could begin building. We never wrote a letter or made a phone call asking for money. We believed that God would supply in His own way and time. We did the groundwork and fencing, dug the lake, built the pavilion, the barn, three cabins, the office, and the pioneer place, and were about to start on the main lodge. We had lived in our Prevost Bus for 13 years and were now going to have a home. We were very excited about getting started.

Our home church in Augusta had a campaign going on to raise money to build a new auditorium debt-free. Our pastor asked me to bring a challenge to the congregation about giving. Not equal gifts but equal sacrifice. It was a great day, and God visited our fellowship, even Billie Kaye and me. We were burdened that we needed to make a sacrificial gift to the building program. We were both led to the same conclusion. Our bus was paid for, and God said, "Give it." So, we did.

We figured it was worth at least $100,000 and could easily be sold. We tried to sell the bus for three months, but not one offer was given. We were starting on the main lodge in two weeks and had enough money for phase one, about $140,000. One night when we were praying, I had a sense that the enemy was trying to rob us of the blessing and the church of the gift for the building. So, I turned to Billie and said, "I believe we should delay the lodge and give the money we pledged." She totally agreed.

The next day, with great joy in our hearts, we sent a check to the church for $100,000. We had only dreamed of doing something like that one day, and now that day had come. It's not that we had or have a lot of money; we just have a source that can never run dry—God Himself. Friend, within two days after we sent that check, the Lord sold the bus, and someone sent a large check that would cover phase two.

I say that story not to brag on our faith or even our obedience, but on the faithfulness of God. You cannot outgive, outthink, out-forgive, or out-love Him. He's the extravagant God who supplies in abundance all our needs according to His riches in glory through Christ Jesus.

I encourage you to make a personal daily declaration of abundance:

- I am a child of the King. The Bible declares I am a member of a royal priesthood; therefore, I have royal blood flowing through my veins. I will begin today by thinking like royalty—not a pauper.
- I will begin today by thanking God for all of His blessings. I will stop complaining about what I don't have and rejoice in what I do have. I am not a victim of my circumstances; I am a victorious warrior over them.
- Abundance is mine today, right now, and always. As my heavenly Father pours abundance into my lap, I will become a hilarious giver and a conduit to others. I declare this in Jesus's name. Amen!

12

STAND YOUR GROUND!

We would worry less if we praised more. Thanksgiving is the enemy of discontent and dissatisfaction.

—Harry Ironside[1]

Many states have a "Stand Your Ground" law. This law has become controversial in recent years because circumstances are not always the same, and the law can be challenging to interpret. Simply said, when someone feels his or her life is in danger, the law allows the threatened person to take all necessary means to defend themselves, including lethal force.

My purpose is not to add to the controversy but to remind you that you have the spiritual right to stand your ground when confronted by the enemy. As the apostle Paul says, *"Having done all, stand!"* (Ephesians 6:13).

FIGHT OR FLIGHT?

The fight-or-flight response, also known as the acute stress response, is a physiological reaction that occurs when confronted with something mentally or physically terrifying. American physiologist Walter Cannon first described the fight-or-flight response in the 1920s. Cannon realized that a chain of

> rapidly occurring reactions inside the body helps mobilize the body's resources to deal with threatening circumstances.
>
> In response to acute stress, the body's sympathetic nervous system is activated due to the sudden release of hormones. The sympathetic nervous system stimulates the adrenal glands, triggering the release of catecholamines, including adrenaline and noradrenaline. This results in an increase in heart rate, blood pressure, and breathing rate. After the threat is gone, it takes between 20 and 60 minutes for the body to return to its pre-arousal levels.
>
> Essentially, the response prepares the body to either fight or flee the threat. It is also important to note that the response can be triggered due to both real and imaginary threats.[2]

Whether you like it or not, you will go through tough times. Whether you collapse or stand your ground is a decision you must make. Whether you are the bravest person on earth or whether you become the most terrified of them all.

So why feel afraid? If you will pass through these tough times anyway, why not pass through them like a warrior? The choice is yours. The outcome may be the same. How do you want to be remembered? In short, if you are going through tough conditions, live like a lion. As one of our past presidents said, "The only thing we have to fear is fear itself."

WILL YOU CHOOSE TO FIGHT BACK OR GIVE IN TO WORRY AND FEAR?

Remember, taking the right weapons when going into battle is essential. David faced Goliath with five smooth stones, not a spear or sword. Why? He knew that conventional weapons would never win the fight. So it is in this war with worry. If what you've been doing so far hasn't worked with conventional weapons, it's time to try something different.

Remember, you are not alone! In your instruction manual (the Bible), God has already provided powerful weapons and positive strategies to win the war over worry.

In a brief passage of Scripture, the apostle Paul offers three powerful weapons to strike a death blow to worry and fear. Philippians 4:4-9 (NIV) tells us:

> ***Rejoice in the Lord always***. *I will say it again: Rejoice! Let your gentleness be evident to all. The Lord is near. Do not be anxious about anything, but* ***in every situation, by prayer*** *and petition, with thanksgiving, present your requests to God. And the peace of God, which transcends all understanding, will guard your hearts and your minds in Christ Jesus. Finally, brothers and sisters, whatever is true, whatever is noble, whatever is right, whatever is pure, whatever is lovely, whatever is admirable—if anything is excellent or praiseworthy—think about such things. Whatever you have learned or received or heard from me, or seen in me—put it into practice. And* ***the God of peace will be with you***.

1. THE WEAPON OF PRAISE.

"Rejoice in the Lord always. I will say it again: Rejoice!"

Praise is celebrating God as our heart's true home. Praise includes commending, expressing approval, or a favorable judgment of, and glorifying, especially by crediting with perfections (Merriam-Webster's dictionary, "praise").

The Scriptures are filled with injunctions to praise the Lord:

- 1 Chronicles 29:20
- Psalm 113:1
- Psalm 117:1

- Psalm 150:6
- And so many more!

Praise puts God in first place. Praise is turning our attention away from ourselves to focus on God. Praise is remembering and recounting who He is and what He has done. Praise keeps us from wallowing in the mire of worry and self-pity.

The essence of praise is simply bragging about God. Praise keeps our problems in perspective. We can view problems as minor and God as big, or we view problems big and God small—the choice is up to us.

There is a story in the Bible about two men who had a lot to worry about. Their names were Paul and Silas. In an unforeseen circumstance, they found themselves deep inside a Philippian jail. (See Acts 16.)

These two men had been arrested for the good deed of casting a spirit of divination out of a young slave girl. After a brief trial, they were beaten with rods and placed in the innermost dungeon with their feet in stocks. How did they respond? Did they complain? Fill the atmosphere with worry and negativity? No, they sang hymns of praise to God at midnight instead of crying themselves to sleep. They made the exceptional choice to praise, not to worry.

What would most people have done in such circumstances? We probably would have groaned and complained about how unfair the day's circumstances were. Paul and Silas didn't gripe about the darkness, the slimy moss on the walls, or the rats they could hear and feel. What did they do? Paul looked at Silas and said, "Let's praise the Lord!"

Luke tells us that while they sang, the other prisoners were listening to them; no doubt they were! The other prisoners had heard many things before, but never sounds like this. God responded to their remarkable faith by delivering them from the dungeon of despair, discouragement, and worry. *"The foundations of the prison were shaken, and immediately all the doors were open, and everyone's chains were loosed"* (Acts 16:26 NKJV). Not only were they delivered, but the Roman soldier who oversaw the prison accepted salvation along with many others in his household!

Paul and Silas refused to magnify the negative situation. They did not analyze their trouble with a magnifying glass, which always leads to discouragement; instead, they magnified the Lord with their praise.

You may find yourself at the "midnight hour" of your prison of worry. God may not seem close to you right now. Please know that your feelings will lie to you. It's easy to complain when faced with things that frighten you or circumstances that seem to go from bad to worse. Nevertheless, if you want God to come into your midnight hour, you must resist the temptation to murmur and complain.

Opening your mouth and speaking praise may sound hard. I know from personal experience that the last thing you want to do is praise when it's so much easier to worry.

Praise is a conscious choice and act of your will. When you offer God praise, you consciously commend, approve, and glorify Him. Praise, therefore, is not based on emotions or feelings. You may have the worst day of your life (remember Paul and Silas) and still choose to praise Him. Deep down inside you know that God is in your corner. Never allow your troubles to keep you from praising the Lord!

Find every verse of Scripture that speaks of praise and begin your day by reading them out loud. Some people start the day by saying, "Good Lord, it's morning." If you're one of those, turn it around and start your day by saying, "Good morning, Lord. This is going to be the best day of my life!"

One of the most remarkable series of messages I've ever preached that God used in a mighty way to change the hearts of His people is titled "The Priority of Praise." I recently re-recorded these messages for my edification. Praise is one of the most powerful weapons in our arsenal. Remember, it's a choice.

Let me help you start your day with a favorite passage, Psalm 149.

I encourage you to read Psalm 149 (NIV) out loud now and whenever you need a surge of positivity:

Praise the Lord.
Sing to the Lord a new song,
his praise in the assembly of his faithful people.
Let Israel rejoice in their Maker;
let the people of Zion be glad in their King.
Let them praise his name with dancing
and make music to him with timbrel and harp.
For the Lord takes delight in his people;
he crowns the humble with victory.
Let his faithful people rejoice in this honor
and sing for joy on their beds.
May the praise of God be in their mouths
and a double-edged sword in their hands,
to inflict vengeance on the nations
and punishment on the peoples,
to bind their kings with fetters,
their nobles with shackles of iron,
to carry out the sentence written against them—
this is the glory of all his faithful people.
Praise the Lord.

Praise brings God into your daily environment. God is the same whether you praise Him or not; His day is not determined by how much you praise Him. If my praise does not change God, who does the praise affect?

- Praise changes and affects you.
- Praise invites God into your day so He can handle whatever comes your way. He inhabits the praise of His people.

- Praise puts flesh to our faith.
- Praise turns impossibilities into victories.

2. THE WEAPON OF PRAYER.

> *Be anxious for nothing, but in everything by prayer and supplication, with thanksgiving let your requests be made known to God* (Philippians 4:6 NKJV).

The Greek word translated as *anxious* (careful) in Philippians 4:6 means "be pulled in different directions." Our hopes and dreams (vision) pull us in one direction; our worries pull us in the opposite direction.

Paul's formula for winning the war over worry includes prayer. His answer goes far beyond positive thinking; it includes effectively connecting with God. In one verse of Scripture, three different Greek words are used to describe prayer.

- The first word translated as *prayer* refers to a general offering up of wishes and desires to God. This points to a mind of devotion and unrestricted dialogue between us and God. It includes adoration, thanksgiving, confession, and intercession.
- The second word translated as *supplication* comes from a Greek word meaning entreaty, seeking, or need. It describes extreme want. To make a supplication means expressing personal needs or a special petition for the supply of wants.
- The third word, translated as *request* refers to things we simply ask of God. It tells us that God is interested in the small things and the big things in our life, but little things left unattended grow up to become big things.

We may think that some things are too insignificant to bring before God, but God tells us that prayer is a two-way conversation between friends. He will never be upset when we make our requests known to Him.

Prayer means I never have to say, "There's nothing I can do." Prayer is the secret weapon of those who connect with the true and living God. It is a guided missile that can be launched toward any place on earth, travel at the speed of thought, and hit its target every time. We do not pray by default because there's nothing else we can do. No. We pray because it is the *best* thing we can do.

Our enemy, satan, has no defense against this weapon of prayer; he does not have an anti-prayer missile.

Now let me ask you a question: if it is true that a genuine believer who is sincerely seeking to live for the Lord can have an effectual prayer life and bring their cares and concerns to the Lord, can they still struggle with anxiety and worry?

The answer is yes! There are several reasons why believers who can pray effectively may still, at times, find themselves anxious.

Let us consider those reasons.

Reason 1: The first reason is that we need to actually enter into God's presence with those cares if we are going to be free of our anxiety: "*... You do not have because you do not ask*" (James 4:2 NKJV).

How often do you pray? I hope your answer is, "I pray a lot." If there were no motivating factor other than our desire to bring all our cares and concerns to the Lord so that we may be free of anxiety, that one motivating factor alone would continually draw us into God's presence.

If you are a believer and know that you sincerely seek to live your life fully and ultimately for the Lord, but you are anxious about something, ask yourself this question, "Have I taken this care or concern to the Lord in prayer?" If you answer "No," you should know your suffering is unnecessary. The solution for your worry is simply a prayer away.

If we fail to pray about our cares and concerns, we can be anxious even if we are true Christians and genuinely desire to live for Him.

However, this is not the only reason a true believer or a person seeking to live for the Lord might experience anxiety.

Reason 2: The second reason is that we must leave those worries with Him to be free from anxiety: *"Cast all your anxiety on him because he cares for you"* (1 Peter 5:7 NIV).

Psalm 55:22 (NIV) says, *"Cast your cares on the Lord, and he will sustain you; he will never let the righteous be shaken."*

Some Christians go into God's presence with their concerns, and they verbalize many wonderful things. Still, their anxiety will not be relieved unless they can trust Him with their anxiety and demonstrate trust by casting their cares upon Him.

If we are able by faith to cast our cares upon Him, believing that He cares for us and that He is perfectly able and willing to manage those cares on our behalf, what would be the appropriate response on our part toward Him? Thanksgiving!

3. THE WEAPON OF PEACE.

Peace is often understood as "calmness or rest," and Jesus frequently spoke of it during His ministry. The term *peace* appears more than 100 times in the New Testament, and almost every instance refers to this inner calm and stillness of the soul. This is precisely how Jesus described it in the passage we're studying.

In John 14, Jesus spoke privately with His disciples, preparing them for what would happen surrounding His crucifixion. In verse 27 (NIV), He says, *"Peace I leave with you; my peace I give to you. I do not give to you as the world gives. Do not let your hearts be troubled and do not be afraid."*

Jesus explains that He would be leaving to prepare a place for them and promised that He would return. While He would be away, He assured them that He would send them the "Helper," Someone with the exact nature and character as His. We know this Helper to be the

Holy Spirit. John 14 shows the deep love and care Jesus had for His disciples and all people.

Now, let's explore the peace Jesus wanted His disciples to have. He highlights three main points here. Remember, this conversation took place right before His crucifixion. Jesus wanted His followers to understand that the Holy Spirit would come soon after His ascension. He knew the challenges they would face after His resurrection, so He promised them a "receipt," so to speak, to help them through difficult and troubled times.

Look at the second part of Jesus's statement, *"I do not give to you as the world gives."*

- In times of difficulty, *His peace will overcome fear and stress.* Fear is a natural response to unexpected trouble. When unsettling events suddenly strike, it is common to feel fear and doubt. I believe that Jesus understood there would be days when His disciples (and we) would doubt, and He was trying to instill peace. He knew they were about to face great turmoil and stress, and the only way to overcome it was to embrace His peace.
- *True peace comes only from God.* What kind of peace can we find in the world? Honestly, not much. People often seek peace through pills, drinks, medications, or even government programs. When we turn on the TV, we hear about peace efforts in places including the Middle East, China, South America, and other parts of the world. It's clear that everyone is searching for peace, but true peace is hard to find. The world offers peace that depends on achievements, material possessions, status, power, or wealth—what some call the "American Dream." I'm not saying there's anything wrong with wanting to succeed or live a good life. I lead a community where I pray for people's success but also for them to find a lasting, more profound peace that goes beyond understanding.

Jesus had a different view of peace than the world offers. He made it clear that the world's search for peace falls short. Nothing the world provides can bring real, lasting peace. The world believes that peace will come if there are no more wars, poverty, or suffering. It thinks peace would exist if all conflicts between people and nations could be resolved.

But real peace doesn't come from getting rid of problems. It doesn't come from peace treaties, international meetings, or disarmament deals. True peace comes from Someone—Jesus Christ, the Prince of Peace.

This means that even amid war, poverty, suffering, or conflict, the peace Jesus brings can be with us. He gives us comfort and strength no matter what we face. Jesus walks with us through every storm and challenging situation, and He promises, *"I will never leave you nor forsake you."* (Hebrews 13:5 NKJV).

What kind of peace does Jesus offer? *"And the peace of God, which transcends all understanding, will guard your hearts and your minds in Christ Jesus"* (Philippians 4:7 NIV).

God's peace can push worry and stress out of our hearts and minds. It doesn't just get rid of anxiety and fear—it keeps them from coming back.

God's peace guards our hearts and minds, keeping worry, hopelessness, and fear from sneaking back in. It is stronger than the anxieties and fears that come naturally to us. Just as God is bigger than any challenge we face, His peace is more potent than any internal fear or stress we might feel. Even in the most challenging and overwhelming situations, we can feel deep and lasting peace. It might seem impossible or hard to believe, so Paul says, *"The peace of God...surpasses all understanding* [comprehension]" (NKJV). This kind of peace is something the world can't give us.

Look again at our text from John 14:27: *"My peace I give you."*

Jesus, knowing the future as clearly as He knew the past, was fully aware of the trials His disciples would soon face. He knew that in a few days, they would be under immense pressure from all sides. The Pharisees would be hunting them, and they would find themselves hiding behind locked doors for safety. He knew they would fall asleep when He asked them to pray with Him in Gethsemane and that they would abandon Him when the soldiers came to arrest Him. He understood that at His trial, He would stand alone.

The guilt and regret the disciples must have felt would have been overwhelming. Imagine the emotions they experienced! They had boldly told Jesus they would never leave Him just days earlier. Peter even declared he would rather die than deny Him, saying in Mark 14:29 (NIV), *"Even if all fall away, I will not,"* and in verse 31, *"Even if I have to die with you, I will never disown you."*

But those brave words did not hold up when the moment came. When Jesus was arrested, the disciples scattered, each one trying to protect himself, gripped by fear and confusion, wondering if everything they had believed was a dream.

Peter, who had boldly boasted, hid in the shadows while Jesus was taken to face Pilate. He worked up the courage to come closer, but when questioned by a servant girl, he denied knowing Jesus. "I don't know what you're talking about," he said, even swearing, "I don't know the man!" He repeated this denial, cursing and swearing each time. (See Mark 14:66-72.)

Except for John, none of the apostles were present until after Jesus was buried. John stayed by the Cross when Jesus was crucified and died. Notably, John was the only apostle who died of old age, while the others met martyrdom.

Despite all their failures and fears, how did Jesus respond? While hiding behind locked doors, he appeared to them and said, *"Peace be with you"* (Luke 24:36). Though they were startled and afraid, thinking they had seen a ghost, Jesus didn't offer rebuke or condemnation. He showed no anger or resentment—only peace and love.

He comforted them by saying, *"Why are you troubled, and why do doubts arise in your minds? Look at my hands and my feet. It is I myself! Touch me and see; a ghost does not have flesh and bones, as you see I have"* (Luke 24:38-39 NIV).

If you find yourself "running on empty," maybe it's time to take steps to do something about it. Christ stands ready and able to do exceedingly abundantly above all you can ask or think. He takes our worst fears and worries and turns them into faith and peace when we lay them down at His feet. Coming to the end of our self and casting our cares on Him is the beginning of a life full of unspeakable joy and peace that passes all understanding. A worry-free life, if you will.

Won't you join me in the tremendous promise of God in 1 Peter 5:7 (KJV), *"Casting all your care upon him: for he careth for you."* He promises that if we do the casting, He'll do the caring.

Are you ready?

Then let's cast away!

13

BEING A MAN IS A FULL-TIME JOB

A FINAL WORD TO MEN

There are no great men of God, only a great God in yielded men.
—Paul E. Tsika

Manhood. What does it truly look like? What defines a man? Is it merely about physical attributes, or is there something deeper? I have long believed that God created us for greatness. The challenge is that many Christian men never experience that greatness. We yearn for it, dream of it, and even attend church or "man" seminars in pursuit of it. Yet, despite the wealth of information available, the books written, and the sermons preached, there appears to be a decline in authentic godly manhood.

I certainly don't have all the answers, but I would like to share a few observations and suggestions. Honestly, I love the idea of manhood. I have two amazing sons who are better fathers, husbands, grandfathers, and godly men than I've ever been. I have them beat, at this point, when it comes to being a better great-grandfather.

I want to share a few words with you and hear your thoughts about each. Ultimately, I ask God to speak to all our hearts as men, empowering us to become men who are yielded to the Holy Spirit and controlled by Him daily.

I've never doubted God's plan for us men, but I have experienced periods of doubt regarding my willingness to submit to His purpose. Oh, I'm not referring to public perception. I've always appeared strong in public. However, those private moments when I'm alone, and only God is watching, have been my struggle, and I'm guessing they've also been yours.

God is calling all men in His Kingdom to become mature, godly men who will live with the mantra, *"As for me and my house, we will serve the Lord"* (Joshua 24:15 KJV).

Boys become true men, not through an accumulation of birthdays, but through a deep work of the Holy Spirit in their lives.

With so many men, they believe that bravado and machismo are what makes a man a man. But most of the time, that's only a cover-up for their own insecurity. It's not about free-scaling El Capitan with only shorts and sneakers or swimming through shark-infested waters with a knife between my teeth.

The words I want you to think about are your commitment, loyalty, character, integrity, faithfulness, and being a protector of all that God has blessed you with.

What the world needs are:

- Men who boldly love and serve Christ.
- Men who act as guardians of their families; they display godly character.
- Men who cannot be swayed by temptation.
- Men who keep their promises and follow through on their commitments.
- Men who prioritize integrity over wealth.
- Men who understand it's not about who's right, but what's right.
- Men who stand firm like a sturdy log, advocating for those who cannot stand for themselves.

- Men who live undeterred by the responsibilities they have been blessed with.
- Men who run their race, finish their course, and keep the faith.

God created men to be as an anchor that secures a large sea vessel. That anchor is unseen by the naked eye when doing what it was created to do. But the effects of that anchor are obvious. *It holds everything in place!*

Storms will come and go, but the anchor of a man filled with God will hold firm in faith until life's storms pass. The apostle Paul states in 1 Corinthians 13:11 (NKJV), *"When I was a child, I spoke as a child, I understood as a child, I thought as a child; but when I became a man, I put away childish things."*

There is (or at least there should be) a noticeable difference between a boy and a man. The problem is that too many grown men with families are acting like boys. Many men I've coached still insist on thinking like children, even though they are married with kids. It's as if they want all the benefits of married life but still wish to live as if they're single—out with the boys, playing video games endlessly, wasting time on what they enjoy while neglecting their wives and children; no dreams, no purpose, and no sense of responsibility for building anything generationally. They have a man's body with a boy's mentality. How about just growing up and accepting your responsibility for your family? Grow up and become the protector, provider, and responsible adult your family needs.

If you still speak, reason, and think like a child, it's time to grow up and become a man. A real man. Not a chest-thumping, loudmouthed braggart who only talks about being a man. Real men don't need to tell anyone they're men; their lives testify to their manhood.

Boys view crisis negatively, leading them to spend their energy avoiding anything that makes them uncomfortable. Men see a crisis as an opportunity to learn, grow, and change. They embrace the crisis, meeting it head-on.

Boys experience mood swings and throw temper tantrums when they don't get their way. They storm out, drive off quickly, slam doors, throw objects, yell and walk away with a victim mentality. It's not my fault, I'm not responsible, don't blame me, and the cycle goes on. They then retreat to the basement to listen to their computer and document their inactivity. But just three thumbs up, and they'll feel better. Grow up already!

Men who are mature have struggles and challenges, hurt and offense, and aggravations as well. But instead of playing the victim card, they rise to the occasion, exercise self-control and restraint, and become victorious.

Boys are consumers and takers; they want to be cared for. They struggle to maintain a job and constantly need rescuing. They require a perpetual mother who feels sorry for them, which enables them to become more of a victim.

Men are producers, providers, and givers. They are caretakers because they want to be. They are mature and responsible enough not to spend their lives making excuses for themselves, knowing that excuses are nothing more than nails used to build a house of failure.

Boys are a patchwork of those they idolize. They are wannabes and copycats. They spend their time in a fantasy world, hoping to identify with anyone or anything that makes them feel worthy and valued.

Real men are comfortable in their own skin. They don't waste time trying to prove their worth to anyone. They understand that their value comes from who they are in Christ and who Christ is in them, not from what they do but from their identity.[1]

There are three stages of growth in life:

1. The *infancy stage* involves a complete inability to care for oneself. During this stage, you require someone to care for you, feed you, and watch over you.
2. Next is the *adolescent stage*, during which you can dress, feed, and generally attend to your needs.

3. Finally, there is the *mature adult stage*. In this stage, you can care for yourself, watch over, and support others.

I'm certainly not putting down being a boy and enjoying that time of life. I used to be one, believe it or not. It was a long time ago, but I still remember. This is a wonderful time of discovery in life. I only want to challenge all of us "men" who are acting like "boys" to put our toys in the toy box, get out of our knickers, and grow up into men God can use to build families and futures.

We need to be men of valor, men of our word, men who are responsible, men of character, men with integrity, men who show kindness, men who provide, men who hunger and thirst for righteousness, and men who honor God.

I've reached the end of my book, yet I still want to share so much. Every time I have a thought that God gives me, a thousand more come to mind. I love imparting any wisdom, knowledge, or truth I've learned, and most of my lessons come from my own failures. I certainly haven't arrived and have a long way to go. I'm on a journey that began in 1971 when Jesus Christ became my personal Lord and Savior. It's been amazing, certainly not all mountaintops. Looking back, there have been more valleys than mountaintops. But that's where I've learned the most important lessons in life.

I learned that there is always so much more because we can never fully understand the depths of God's love, mercy, and grace. Knowing Him in the power of His resurrection and sharing in His suffering has always been the secret desire of my heart. Have I always lived that? No. But since I first met Him, I have prayed that I might truly know Him. Not just know about Him, but know Him.

My dear reader, as I reflect on my life of over 82 years, I am thankful each day for God's incredible patience, correction, guidance, mercy, and love. Still, quite honestly, so much of that time has been spent growing up spiritually.

I wish for you what I never had at a young age—a true, godly mentor. One who will come alongside and *"provoke you to love and good works"* (see Hebrews 10:24 KJV). One who will challenge you without condemning, incentivize you without manipulation, correct you without guilt, teach you without superiority, and love you with patience, kindness, encouragement, and the Father's heart.

All that and more.

However, since you can't spend every day, all day with a mentor, God has invaded your humanity as a Christian with the greatest Counselor and Mentor of all. The blessed Holy Spirit of God lives in you to lead, guide, correct, and empower you as your Heavenly Mentor. As you look to Him, there will be a constant gentle reminder that *you were created for more.*

So be content, but never be satisfied. I love you very much. Please never settle for less than what God has created you for—*more of Him.*

Today, I looked at calendars
I've kept right from the start
And with each passing year I see
Many things that warm my heart.
I look at all the churches
That we've been blessed to serve
When I think of all those open doors
I feel so undeserved.
Each date a distant memory
Some faint, some very strong
But with each date remembering
What was right and what was wrong.
When I tie it all together
With faces I can see
My belief is that our faithful God
Did a work in spite me.

So, to You, God be the glory
As I look at our faded past
You've done what only You can do
And it's more than I can grasp.
I love You, precious Savior
You're always there for me
For You have been my everything
And will be through eternity.

Paul E. Tsika
December 4, 2024

NOTES

CHAPTER 1

1. http://www.quotationspage.com/quote/9308.html#google_vignette; accessed March 8, 2025.
2. Note: This is a compilation of Martha's determination to open a school. To read more about this incredible woman, go to "The miracle in the mountains" by Dr. Stephen Briggs; reprint from *Berry* magazine, Winter 2019-20; https://www.berry.edu/about/_assets/the-miracle-in-the-mountains.pdf; accessed March 8, 2025.
3. "The Touch of the Master's Hand," *AllPoetry;* https://allpoetry.com/The-Touch-of-the-Master's-Hand; accessed March 8, 2025.
4. Myles Munroe, *Understanding Your Potential* (Destiny Image Publishers, 1991), 12.
5. Today in the Word, December 3, 1992; https://www.todayintheword.org/archives/?searchPhrase=James+Whistler+quote&type=&date=&page=14.

CHAPTER 2

1. https://inspirationfeed.com/maya-angelou-quotes/; accessed March 8, 2025.
2. Rick Warren, "Reigniting Your Passion for God," *SermonCentral,* September 22, 2008; https://www.sermoncentral.com/sermons/

reigniting-your-passion-for-god-rick-warren-sermon-on-zeal-127082; accessed March 8, 2025.

3. CityLife Church Melbourne Australia@ https://web.citylife.church/melbourne-city/; accessed March 8, 2025.
4. "It Only Takes a Spark," Kurt Kaiser, 1969.
5. https://lists.thefamouspeople.com/17-famous-people-who-died-broke.php; accessed March 8, 2025.
5. J. Oswald Sanders, *Facing Loneliness* (Our Daily Bread Publishing, June 10, 2014).
6. "Put Off Until Tomorrow," *Our Daily Bread,* February 15, 2009; https://bible.org/illustration/put-until-tomorrow; accessed March 8, 2025.

CHAPTER 3

1. https://www.socratic-method.com/quote-meanings-interpretations/c-s-lewis-failures-are-finger-posts-on-the-road-to-achievement; accessed March 8, 2025.
2. https://www.whatshouldireadnext.com/quotes/denis-waitley-failure-should-be-our-teacher; accessed March 9, 2025.
3. Text of J.K. Rowling's speech, *The Harvard Gazette,* June 5, 2008; https://news.harvard.edu/gazette/story/2008/06/text-of-j-k-rowling-speech/; accessed March 9, 2025.
4. "Famous People Who Found Success Despite Failures," *Get Busy Living,* May 26, 2022; https://getbusylivingblog.com/famous-people-who-found-success-despite-failures/; accessed March 9, 2025.
5. Ibid.
6. Ibid.
7. Ibid.

8. https://www.snopes.com/fact-check/lincoln-character-power/ (Note: This quote has been misattributed to Lincoln for years, but he never uttered or wrote those words or words to that effect. Rather, they were said about him. The original version of the quotation came on January 16, 1883, during a speech in Washington, DC, by the prominent writer and orator Robert Ingersoll.)
9. Laurence Shames, "The Sweet Smell of 'Success' Isn't All That Sweet," *The New York Times,* April 12, 1986; https://www.nytimes.com/1986/04/12/opinion/the-sweet-smell-of-success-isn-t-all-that-sweet.html; accessed March 9, 2025.
10. F.B. Meyer, "Supreme Test of Goodness," *Our Daily Walk;* https://bible.org/illustration/supreme-test-goodness; accessed March 9, 2025.
11. Zig Ziglar as quoted by Hugh B. Sanders, *The Subconscious Diet: It's Not What You Put in Your Mouth; It Is What You Put in Your Mind* (Liberation Press, 2005), 104.

CHAPTER 4

1. Dietrich Bonhoeffer as quoted in *LIFE* magazine (22 April 1957), p. 152; also in *Letters and Papers from Prison* (1967), p. 47; https://en.wikiquote.org/wiki/Time; accessed March 9, 2025.
2. Dieuner Joseph, "The Danger of a Negative Spirit," *Disciple Maker Ministry,* September 7, 2023; https://www.disciplemakerministry.com/post/the-danger-of-a-negative-spirit; accessed March 19, 2025.
3. Danny Thomas quotes, *Cheermeup.net* | Get Inspired, Motivated and Healed by the Best; https://www.cheermeup.net/author/danny-thomas.html; accessed March 19, 2025.

4. Paul Simkins, "Ten Signs You Need Leadership Development, Part II," *Boldly Lead;* https://www.boldlylead.com/ten-signs-you-should-invest-in-leadership-development-part-ii/; accessed March 19, 2025.
5. Abdul Ghafoor Parekh, "Time Contradiction," *Explore Al Qur'an;* https://explore-quran.com/articles/TimeContradiction.html; accessed March 19, 2025.

CHAPTER 5

1. https://en.wikiquote.org/wiki/Winston_Churchill; accessed March 10, 2025.
2. Harold S. Davis, "The Secret Revealed: Success Is Not Easy," *Foundation for Economic Education,* May 1, 1977; https://fee.org/articles/the-secret-revealed-success-is-not-easy/; accessed March 10, 2025.
3. https://www.merriam-webster.com/dictionary/perspective; accessed March 10, 2025.
4. Terry Orlick, *In Pursuit of Excellence* (Human Kinetics Pub, 2016), 27.
5. Steven K. Scott, *The Richest Man Who Ever Lived* (Crown Publishing, 2006), 32.
6. *The American Alpine Club,* 1969; https://publications.americanalpineclub.org/articles/12196949602/James-Thomas-Madsen-1947-1968; accessed March 10, 2025.
7. Henry L. Allen, Sr., "The Dangers of the Religious Person," *Warriors Rising up for Christ,* July 16, 2023; https://www.gospeltabernaclembchurch.com/post/the-dangers-of-the-religious-person; accessed March 10, 2025.

8. "Treasures from Tozer"; https://www.gracegems.org/29/treasures_from_tozer.htm; accessed March 10, 2025.

CHAPTER 6

1. https://en.wikiquote.org/wiki/George_S._Patton quoted in "The True Story of The Patton Prayer" by James H. O'Neill in *Review of the News* (October 6, 1971).
2. Alan Axelrod, *Patton on Leadership: Strategic Lessons for Corporate Warfare* (Prentice Hall, 1999).
3. http://www.worldofproverbs.com/2012/05/girl-who-cant-dance-says-band-cant-play.html
4. https://marvinduncombe.wixsite.com/marvinduncombe/our-mission; accessed March 11, 2025.
5. Todd Duncan, *The Power to Be Your Best!* (Thomas Nelson, 1999), 35.
6. "20 Notable People Who Dropped Out of School," *How Stuff Works,* August 2, 2022; https://people.howstuffworks.com/15-notable-people-who-dropped-out-of-school.htm; accessed March 11, 2025.
7. Malcolm Gladwell, *Outliers: The Story of Success* (Little, Brown and Co., 2008), 36.
8. Burke Hedges, *You, Inc. Discover the CEO Within* (Blackstone Worldwide Inc., 1996), 25.

CHAPTER 7

1. https://en.wikiquote.org/wiki/Aiden_Wilson_Tozer
2. Myles Munroe, *In Pursuit of Purpose* (Destiny Image Publications, 2015).

3. https://www.jimrohn.com/change-begins-with-choice/
4. Nicholas West, "The 10 Inventions Of Nikola Tesla That Changed The World," *The Millennium Report,* January 14, 2016; https://themillenniumreport.com/2016/01/the-10-inventions-of-nikola-tesla-that-changed-the-world/; accessed March 13, 2025.
5. Mary Bellis, "Inventors: Geore Washington Carver," *theinventors.org,* 2006; http://theinventors.org/library/weekly/aa041897.htm; accessed March 13, 2025.
6. "About Beng Tremendous," *Tremendous Leadership;* https://tremendousleadership.com/pages/charlie; accessed March 13, 2025.

CHAPTER 8

1. *Christian Quotes;* https://www.christianquotes.info/quotes-by-topic/quotes-about-wisdom/#google_vignette; accessed March 13, 2025.
2. "Sermons on Job—Lowell Johnson, *Precept Austin,* January 30, 2021; https://www.preceptaustin.org/job-sermons-lowell-johnson; accessed March 13, 2025.
3. "Pursuing Divine Wisdom," *Grace to You,* January 26, 1996; https://www.gty.org/library/sermons-library/TMU135/pursuing-divine-wisdom; accessed March 13, 2025.
4. Armistice Day speech, 11 November 1948, published in Omar Bradley's Collected Writings; https://en.wikiquote.org/wiki/Omar_Bradley; accessed March 13, 2025.
5. "Words of Wisdom—Man as Provider," *Stand Courageous;* https://standcourageous.com/devoaug2523; accessed March 13, 2025.
6. Tim Kimmel, *Little House on the Freeway* (Waterbrook Multnomah, 2008), 143.

CHAPTER 9

1. Winston Churchill speech at Harrow School, Harrow, England, October 29, 1941. Winston S. Churchill: His Complete Speeches, 1897–1963, ed. Robert Rhodes James, vol. 6, p. 6499 (1974); https://en.wikiquote.org/wiki/Perseverance; accessed March 14, 2025.
2. David Wilkerson, *When You Come to the End of Yourself*; https://sermons-online.org/david-wilkerson/when-you-come-to-the-end-of-yourself; accessed March 14, 2025.
3. Brian Bill, "Nehemiah Sermons," *Precept Austin,* September 10, 2000; https://www.preceptaustin.org/nehemiah_sermons; accessed March 14, 2025.

CHAPTER 10

1. https://medium.com/@thebriantracy/20-brian-tracy-leadership-quotes-for-success-inspiration-5e740c44ffb5; accessed March 14, 2025.
2. https://www.sermonillustrations.com/a-z/p/problems.htm; accessed March 14, 2025.
3. https://evirtualguru.com/essayparagraph-or-speech-on-necessity-is-the-mother-of-invention-complete-paragraph-or-speech-for-class-10-class-12-and-graduation-and-other-classes/; accessed March 14, 2025.
4. https://www.chegg.com/homework-help/questions-and-answers/read-carefully-following-case-study-answer-questions-following-structured-approach-structu-q59197717; accessed March 14, 2025.

5. https://www.chegg.com/homework-help/questions-and-answers/case-study-1-southwest-airlines-airline-survive-government-order-ground-entire-fleet-shut--q41779238
6. "Peter Drucker on Asking the Wrong Questions," *Bard College,* September 9, 2015; https://hac.bard.edu/amor-mundi/peter-drucker-on-asking-the-wrong-questions-2015-09-29; accessed March 14, 2025.
7. "The Doctrine of the 10 Problem-Solving Devices," *Robert R. McLaughlin Bible Ministries, Grace Bible Church,* July 2013; https://gbible.org/wp-content/uploads/2013/07/Doctrine-of-Problem-Solving-Devices.pdf; accessed March 14, 2025.
8. Mike Murdock, *1 Minute Businesswoman's Devotional* (Wisdom International, Inc., 2012), 195.

CHAPTER 11

1. https://www.allgreatquotes.com/authors/ben-sweetland/; accessed March 18, 2025.
2. Stephen R. Covey, A. Roger Merrill, Rebecca R. Merrill, *First Things First* (Free Press, 2003).
3. Senior Living Ministries; https://www.seniorlivingministries.org/2016/11/believing-in-gods-abundance/; accessed March 18, 2025.

CHAPTER 12

1. https://www.christianquotes.info/quotes-by-topic/quotes-about-praise/; accessed March 18, 2025.
2. Kendra Cherry, "What Is the Fight-or-Flight Response?, *Very Well Mind,* June 17, 2024; https://www.verywellmind.com/what-is-the-fight-or-flight-response-2795194; accessed March 18, 2025.

CHAPTER 13

1. Excerpts from "Endangered Species Mature Men" by Junior DeSouza by permission. https://www.patheos.com/blogs/robertricciardelli/faith/endangered-species-mature-men-by-junior-desouza/; accessed March 19, 2025.

ABOUT PAUL E. TSIKA

Paul and Billie Kaye Tsika have been involved in ministry for almost 50 years. He has authored several books including: *What You Seed Is What You Get; Sequoia-Size Success; Releasing Your Full Potential;* and *The Overcomer's Edge.* Together they have authored books including: *Growing in Favor; Get Married, Stay Married;* and *Parenting with Purpose.* Paul has been the pastor of a large international marketing business since 2001. Along with their staff, they minister to tens of thousands of people each year and witness many coming to Christ for salvation. They reside at Restoration Ranch in Texas.